JOINED

by

GOD

Unconventional Devotions for Christian Couples

SHELLIE ARNOLD

Kaleidoscope Publishing
Reflecting God's Truth

Joined by God by Shellie Arnold
Published by Kaleidoscope Publishing
A division of Purple Umbrella LLC
1738 Oak Trail St. NE, Massillon, OH 44646

Print ISBN: 979-8-9893127-1-9 | ISBN: 979-8-9893127-2-6
Copyright © 2024 by Shellie Arnold
Cover design by Stephanie Arnold and Shellie Arnold
Interior design by Kaleidoscope Publishing

Available in print from your local bookstore, online, or from the publisher
at www.kaleidoscopebooks.net and www.shelliearnoldbooks.com and
www. shelliearnold.com and www.sevenweekdevos.com.

Library of Congress Cataloging-in-Publication Data: Arnold, Shellie.
Joined by God / Shellie Arnold 1st ed.

Printed in the United States of America

PRAISE FOR *JOINED BY GOD: UNCONVENTIONAL DEVOTIONS FOR CHRISTIAN COUPLES*

This seven-week tool provides provocative and practical applications to you as individuals and as a couple. Shellie's candor and insights help you examine the "whys" of your motivation as you seek to become a better "us" in your marriage! We highly recommend the investment for every couple seeking to grow closer in their love for one another.

~ Bill and Pam Mutz, FamilyLife Weekend to Remember speakers, married forty-seven years

Most of us head into marriage with our belongings, lofty dreams, unrealistic expectations—and all the baggage of our lives up until our wedding day. That can impact our marriages in ways we never anticipated. In *Joined by God: Unconventional Devotions for Christian Couples,* my sweet friend Shellie Arnold shares biblical wisdom, inspiration, and valuable tips to help us achieve stronger marriages and happier homes. I highly recommend this book.

~ Michelle Cox, wife of forty-nine years, bestselling author of *Hope That Endures: 40 Devotions of Encouragement for Difficult Times, Our Daily Biscuit: Devotions with a Drawl,* and the *When God Calls the Heart* series of devotional books

Shellie Arnold says it best: "To build a healthy marriage, we must start and end with God." Whether your marriage needs a fresh coat of paint or a new foundation, this book has just what you need to strengthen your marriage while cultivating your relationship with the ultimate marriage coach, the Heavenly Father. As Arnold says, "A thriving, healthy marriage depends on understanding God's character and how

He loves, then duplicating those habits in marriage." A much-needed resource for couples!

~ Julie Lavender, wife of forty years, mom to four, mom-in-law to two, grand mommy to one, and author of *Children's Bible Stories for Bedtime* and *Strength for All Seasons: A Mom's Devotional of Powerful Verses and Prayers.*

Shellie's quick wit will draw you in to these unconventional devotions. In *Joined by God*, she delivers truths, sometimes hard ones, with genuineness and love, while offering encouragement and practical ways to grow in your marriage, and more importantly, in your relationship with God. This isn't a one-time-through kind of book, but one that couples should consider picking up and working through again and again. Thank you, Shellie, for offering such sage advice for married couples.

~ Edwina Perkins, wife of thirty-five years, co-director of the Blue Ridge Mountains Christian Writers Conference, managing editor for Harambee Press, manager for Sensitivity Between the Lines, freelancer for Guideposts

If you're looking for something to take your marriage to the next level, or heal past hurts, or solidify God's best for your marriage—you're holding it. Shellie shares tested truth straight from Scripture in a transparent manner. She promises and delivers hope and relationship principles, to take your marriage far beyond being okay or even healthy. Following these principles can truly help you and your mate flourish the way God intended.

~ Tina Hunt, wife of forty-five years, pastor, author

Joined by God: Unconventional Devotions for Christian Couples is not your typical devotional. This book is a combination devotional, workbook, and journal. Shellie Arnold bypasses clichés, providing content to chew and meditate on, whether you read this with your spouse or alone. Warning: Do not read *Joined by God* unless you want to improve your own relationship with God *and* improve your marriage as a direct result!

~ Ava Pennington, wife of forty years, Bible study teacher, speaker, and author of *Reflections on the Names of God: 180 Devotions to Know God More Fully*

I'm not tossing out hyperbole when I say, *Joined by God* will transform the marriage of any couple who works through this devotional and heeds the biblical truths Shellie Arnold shares. Even if only one spouse embraces the content in Arnold's short, conversational style devotions, the change in perspective can lead to a transformed heart and a stronger marriage.

~ Jean Wilund, wife of thirty-eight years, author of *Embracing Joy: An 8-Week Transformational Bible Study of Habakkuk*

About This Book
(and how to use it)

Write the book you're looking for, I once heard while attending a writers conference. That was all the permission I needed to start brainstorming a series of devotionals for couples. I wanted to offer resources that help readers sink deep into Scripture and find its treasure. Ones with short, yet still thought-provoking, daily readings. Books flexible enough to promote spiritual growth and intimacy in a couple even if only one spouse read them. Books that help create the habit of sharing what God is doing in our individual lives, so we can enjoy the fruit of that work in our marriages. And I hoped to provide easy ways to tie it all together at the end of each week. This combination led to the subtitle *Unconventional Devotions for Christian Couples.*

You'll notice each week highlights a particular Scripture passage. You'll be prompted to read the passage each day. I urge you to complete this step. The investment will bring huge dividends in your spiritual walk and marriage. The daily readings focus on various topics, truths, or issues.

The *Just for You* sections offer questions to process and apply the daily reading content in light of God's character and additional Scripture. Each day ends with *For Your Marriage* prompts to immediately share with your mate all God is speaking to you.

The weeks end with a *Quick Connection for the Weekend* where you'll find the opportunity not only to review, but also to plan action steps for continued implementation of all God is revealing to you. Simply bring it up after breakfast, or right before bed, or even while driving to church—the options are endless. The goal is to engage about spiritual matters, to ponder scriptural truths, and make praying together a regular part of your marriage.

Lastly, if your mate is open to working through this book together, that's fabulous! If your mate is hesitant, downright resistant, or your schedules become insane, that's okay. I've been there. If you get

behind, or forget, or lose it for a month that's okay, too. Simply start where you left off. God is with you in this season, He is anxious to interact with you, and He is ready to do a miraculous work in your marriage.

TABLE OF CONTENTS

Before you begin ...

Hey there! Chances are we haven't met, yet you're about to join me on a journey I embarked on decades ago. Go, us!

To be clear, I'm not a counselor, therapist, psychologist, or even a pastor's wife. I'm a kid from a broken home who wanted absolutely nothing to do with marriage. After watching my parents' marriage end in divorce, by the time I was fifteen I was certain I didn't want to get married.

Then God made clear He was leading me toward marriage. He *called* me to marriage. I have no other way to describe it.

God called me to marriage and scared me to my bones. I didn't want to get married and get hurt. I didn't want to get married and fall out of love with my husband. I had seen divorce from the kid's side, and the possibility of going through that pain from the adult's side terrified me.

Let me back up. I met my husband at school during the eighth grade. No, we didn't fall instantly in love. Rather, he thought I was stuck up, and I thought he was just a mean eighth-grade boy—which he was. One day during lunch, he and his friends were teasing a fellow classmate. After, I saw her crying in the bathroom. Since his locker was beside mine, I took advantage of us both getting books between classes to tell him how mean he was. Then, somehow, we became friends. For the next year or so, he dated many girls including some of my friends, which was fine with me. I didn't care he was looking for a future wife.

While Stephen dated around, I dropped out of youth group at our church to attend all the marriage classes. Surrounded by couples young and old, I watched the videos, read the books, and took notes. I learned some of what a healthy marriage should look like, but I wasn't told how to actually build one, why I should try, or where to find answers when tough times came and conflicts arose. Consequently, I decided not to marry. I figured there wasn't a way to be married and not hurt each other, or if there *was* a way … it was a secret God refused to share.

At age fifteen when Stephen's eyes focused on me—well, to say I was petrified is an understatement. Fifteen-year-olds don't stay friends after they break up. I was convinced after a couple of weeks of "going together" he would meet the petite blonde of his dreams (I am neither petite nor blonde). Then he would break up with me, and I would lose him as my friend.

I didn't want to lose him as my friend. As a result of my parents' divorce, I'd lost so much already. But Stephen stuck around. He didn't go away, and then he *really* didn't go away. He told me he was going to marry me.

And I began to pray about the love God was growing in my heart for a guy who wanted to marry me even though he knew I wasn't getting married, and he knew why. We were friends, remember? He'd witnessed firsthand much of the fallout and consequences of my parents' divorce, right down to the little suitcase I lugged to school and church as I went back and forth between homes.

When that love continued to grow, I knew I had a decision to make. Either walk away from Stephen, and therefore, walk away from where I knew God was leading me, or walk with God into the most emotionally dangerous place I could imagine—a marriage.

If you've ever witnessed a child being dropped off at daycare or school and seen them desperately clinging to their parent because they don't want to be left behind, you have a tiny glimpse of how I felt inside about agreeing to marry Stephen. I pretty much wrapped my arms around God's knees and told Him I couldn't do what He wanted me to do unless He stayed with me and promised to teach me.

And you know what? God promised me exactly that, and He has kept His promise. He started with baby steps, and He continues to walk me through healing from trauma in my childhood, including sexual abuse. He continues to transform my life by renewing my mind with Scripture and truth. He teaches me how to think differently, so I can live differently. He confronts bad habits I learned when I was

young, challenges me about my blind spots, and convicts me when I am clueless about my own spiritual rebellion.

Through thirty-seven plus years of marriage, God has stayed with me even when I didn't feel Him, didn't recognize Him, and didn't believe He was there. Even when I was disillusioned with Him, and so angry I refused to pray or listen. With each breath I learn more, see more, grow more, and believe more about Him and His plan for marriage.

To be clear, there is scriptural provision for righteous divorce. God doesn't command we stay in a marriage where abuse or addictions create an unsafe environment. And none of us can make our mate do the right thing. If someone wants to leave us, cheat, or walk away from God, we can't stop them.

Yet God has much provision for those who will pursue Him. This devotional is me sharing with you what I've learned the hard way. Stuff I wish someone had told me before I married, or that I'd learned sooner. It's what I've learned slowly with God's help when there was so much for me to learn.

You'll find I don't share a lot of fluffy stories. I will challenge you to embrace personal accountability with your Savior, because that is where God the Father pushes me.

One of the greatest traumas of my life, my parents' divorce, became the basis for my calling to help marriages. I want to share everything God has taught me and continues to teach me about having a healthy, growing marriage.

Here's something I want you to remember:

**Jesus died to redeem every part of your life.
You can experience His redemption in every
part of your marriage.**

Did you get that? Jesus didn't die so you and I could experience wimpy love or a mediocre marriage. He died to redeem, heal, and restore our lives to what God originally intended us to have from the beginning in the Garden of Eden.

He will help us. He will lead us. He will teach us if we listen. My favorite verses are Isaiah 1:18–19:

"*18*Come now, let us reason together, says the Lord: though your sins are like scarlet, they shall be as white as snow; though they are red like crimson, they shall become like wool. *19*If you are willing and obedient, you shall eat the good of the land;"

God will even discuss our sin with us when we approach Him with a willingness to turn from that sin and be obedient in the future. He invites us to converse with Him. I pray this devotional stirs in you a hunger for God, increased love for your mate, and a vision for sharing with others all you learn. So they can also experience the benefits of being Joined by God. Here we go. Woo-hoo!

FOUNDATIONS

Scriptures for this Week (Ephesians 5:21–33)

[21] ... submitting to one another out of reverence for Christ. [22] Wives, submit to your own husbands, as to the Lord. [23] For the husband is the head of the wife even as Christ is the head of the church, his body, and is himself its Savior. [24] Now as the church submits to Christ, so also wives should submit in everything to their husbands. [25] Husbands, love your wives, as Christ loved the church and gave himself up for her, [26] that he might sanctify her, having cleansed her by the washing of water with the word, [27] so that he might present the church to himself in splendor, without spot or wrinkle or any such thing, that she might be holy and without blemish. [28] In the same way husbands should love their wives as their own bodies. He who loves his wife loves himself. [29] For no one ever hated his own flesh, but nourishes and cherishes it, just as Christ does the church, [30] because we are members of his body. [31] 'Therefore a man shall leave his father and mother and hold fast to his wife, and the two shall become one flesh.' [32] This mystery is profound, and I am saying that it refers to Christ and the church. [33] However, let each one of you love his wife as himself, and let the wife see that she respects her husband.

Week One, Day One

Our Greatest Calling

My marriage is about much more than me and my husband. *Your* marriage is about much more than you and your mate. Or making a home for your children.

As believers, our marriages are supposed to point others to God and His love for them. I know that doesn't sound very romantic. I risk you tossing this book aside and never again picking it up.

But I care about your marriage and family too much to *not* tell you the truth. Because you're reading this book, I can guess your heart for your marriage and any children you have. You want your marriage to flourish, and you want to point your children to God in all you do. And the truth is, your family and children are watching, just as the world is watching. One day when those children leave your home and become part of the world outside your home, they'll still be watching.

As individuals who love God and want to follow Him, we must consider the long-term effects of what others see—especially our children and those who don't know God—in our marriages. As the Church, as believers, we must consider why so often those outside the Church don't believe God loves them, and what we can do about it.

Ready?

While there are many reasons those outside the Church don't believe God loves them—evil they see in the world, pain they and those they care about experience, and other evidence they interpret as proof of God's absence or neglect—there's one tool every married believer can use to minister to every person we encounter.

A healthy, growing marriage.

Most of us are familiar with the passage at the end of Ephesians 5. Still, I challenge you to carefully read it again and look for these six phrases:

"as to the Lord" (verse 22)

"as Christ is the head of the church" (verse 23)

"as the church submits to Christ" (verse 24) "as Christ loved the church" (verse 25)

"in the same way" (verse 28)

"as Christ does the church" (verse 29).

As you can see, a godly, growing marriage is the primary witnessing tool the Church has today. Our marriages can literally show others how God loves His children.

Don't get me wrong. I understand there is scriptural provision for righteous divorce. There are circumstances in which it would be sinful to stay in a marriage, such as when there's abuse of spouse or children, or addictions that bring danger into the home.

Still, ask any unbeliever. Ask any person, young or old, who thinks Scripture and the Church are both hooey (yes, it's a word). Eventually they will mention infidelity, adultery, even child abuse or some other sin they've seen among believers. Or the divorce rate among Christians. Or that many couples who claim to be believers don't really love each other, maybe even can't stand each other, and every person who knows them knows it.

The bottom line? Here's a tough truth and reality check. The world doesn't believe God loves them because they see the condition of our marriages and families. They see when we don't love each other. When we are unfaithful. When we lie. When we are unkind. When we withhold love, don't listen, or place our spouses as our last priority. They see when we stop trying.

We, who claim the name of Christ. We, who proclaim God is love, too often aren't loving to each other. The world sees it. Our kids see it. Our personal testimony suffers and with it the testimony of the Church at large.

If I want to witness to a society that's bound by lust and hatred, to those who are slaves to their own wounds and pain and ignorance, there's an easy way.

Grow my marriage. My marriage is supposed to be a living demonstration of Christ and His love.

If I want a dear friend, a beloved family member, a neighbor or co-worker to come to Christ, I have access to a witnessing tool that doesn't require clever speeches or handing someone a gospel tract. I can strengthen my marriage. My marriage is supposed to show the world the power, passion, and pursuing qualities of God's love.

Don't we want our children to see and believe God loves them? That He can do anything? Heal anything? That His love is powerful and transforming and covers a multitude of sins? That God's grace is bigger than every sin He knew we'd commit?

We can show them all this and more is true by cultivating our marriages. Our marriages can prove God's love is present and active in our everyday lives.

Ready for some radical ideas? Prayerfully consider making the following changes so growth or healing can take place in your marriage.

This month, instead of sending extra money to a ministry, invest it in your marriage. For counseling or therapy, a retreat, or great resources and teaching.

This year, instead of taking a ten-day mission trip, give that time to your marriage. To reconnect, refocus, maybe heal and recalibrate.

For the next few months, instead of attending a weekly Bible study or prayer meeting praying for and encouraging others, spend that time praying for and encouraging your mate.

I know these suggestions sound strange. Giving offerings, going on mission trips, and attending Bible studies can all be good things. Yet, depending on where you are in your marriage, are they the best ways to spend your money, energy, and time?

See, days turn into weeks, turn into months, turn into years, and the things we let grow—whether good or bad—will grow or die because of the time and effort we invest in them. If your marriage is strong, don't you want it to be stronger? If your marriage is gasping for breath, shouldn't you give it CPR?

Let those in the world around you, those in your extended family, your children—let them see God working miracles as He works them in you and your marriage. Let them see God's love in action through how you treat your spouse. Let them see the changes, watch your love grow, and feel the difference of "before" versus "after."

That's proof which cannot be refuted. And when someone asks (or if you're like me, even when they don't) you can say "God's love is real. God's love grows. And God's love is for you."

They might not believe it, but because they're watching you, they won't be able to argue with it.

Just for You

Think—reread this week's Scripture passage. God's plan is to use your marriage to demonstrate the power of His love to you and others.

What does this truth imply about the importance of your marriage to God?

_____

_____

_____

Thank God—for His love extended to you.

When has He manifested that love to you?

_____

_____

_____

Take—strength from God's incomprehensible love.

What do you need strength for today? For yourself? For your marriage?

_____

_____

_____

Straight from God

[16] ... that according to the riches of his glory he may grant you to be strengthened with power through his Spirit in your inner being, [17] so that Christ may dwell in your hearts through faith—that you, being rooted and grounded in love, [18] may have strength to comprehend with all the saints what is the breadth and length and height and depth, [19] and to know the love of Christ that surpasses knowledge, that you may be filled with all the fullness of God. (Ephesians 3:16–19)

This passage mentions being "rooted and grounded in love." Spend a few moments letting God's love fill you. How can you show love to your spouse today?

_____

_____

_____

For Your Marriage (choose one or more)

Share today's Straight from God verse with your mate. (Call, text, email, discuss.)

What would you like your mate to pray about for you? (Share.) What can you pray about for your mate? (Ask.)

Share your reaction to the idea God wants your marriage to demonstrate His love for all. (Call, text, or email, discuss.)

Ask God to teach you more about His love for you and listen for His response. (Share, discuss.)

NOTES

_____
_____
_____
_____
_____
_____
_____
_____
_____
_____
_____
_____
_____
_____
_____
_____
_____
_____

Week One, Day Two

Never Without an Example

I know, I know. You might've already heard many sermons on Ephesians 5.

You might be tired of it, leery of it, or both. Hang with me. I promise this week will be worth your time and effort.

Because there's a big deal about Ephesians 5, and it's not what you think. No, I'm not talking about submission. That's for another day, and I can't wait to drop the Submission Bomb on you. You'll never view submission the same way again. In fact, I have every confidence you'll love the idea of submission after hearing my take on it.

But I digress. In yesterday's devotion I pointed out the six phrases like "as to the Lord," "in the same way," and "as Christ does the church" present in Ephesians 5.

Did you come from a broken home? A dysfunctional home? A hypocritical home?

Did you find God later in life? Are you a spiritual infant just getting started in your walk with God, and you know you've made mistakes in your marriage?

Do you have a pretty good marriage, although at times you wish you had a cheat sheet, or a marriage coach right there beside you, for whenever that one conflict comes that always seems to put your marriage on the brink of disaster?

The real big deal about Ephesians 5 is this: We hold the key to having built-in, real-time access to a living example of how to handle our marriages. The example we need is found in our relationship with God.

Think about it. Every time those phrases are mentioned—"as to the Lord," etc.—they're speaking of *our* relationship with God.

How can I learn how to give and receive love in my marriage? Learn to give and receive love in my relationship with God, then copy those habits.

How can I learn to give and receive forgiveness in my marriage? Learn how God forgives, how I receive forgiveness, and again, copy those habits.

My relationship with God isn't simply where I find the strength, love, and steadfastness to stay married to my husband. It's not merely where I find the power and purpose to stand being married one more day.

My relationship with God is my *example*. I learn from it as I live in it.

Every day, every moment, you and I have unlimited, fathomless access to the perfect example of love, loving, and being loved. We find it in our relationship with God.

During the times you don't know what to do in your marriage. When the same issue surfaces over and over and you've hit what appears to be a dead end. When you behave badly and you know you have a mess to clean up, but don't know how. During the times everything is fine, then you're blindsided by catastrophe. During the good times, when you and your beloved are cruising along on the Love Train.

Take a moment. Pay attention and consider—where are you in relation to God? Where is your marriage in relation to God? Does He seem far away? Inattentive? Silent? Is He right there smiling, rejoicing, and singing over you and your spouse?

Then, alone and with your mate, spend time in God's presence.

Waiting on Him. Listening to Him.

Learn to watch for Him and His influence in yourself and in each other.

The example you need when facing the next big challenge, or the challenge you're in now, is right there with you. You never have to feel stuck or stagnant again.

Just for You

Think—reread this week's Scripture passage. You are never alone in your marriage.

How can this truth help you every day?

_____

_____

_____

Thank God—you are never without the best example for your marriage.

In what areas of your marriage do you need to emulate Jesus? In what areas of your life?

_____

_____

_____

Take—comfort in the truth you are never without guidance to strengthen your marriage.

How can this comfort help you rest in God today?

_____

_____

_____

Straight from God

"Take my yoke upon you, and learn from me, for I am gentle and lowly in heart, and you will find rest for your souls." (Matthew 11:29)

This verse mentions finding rest as we learn from Jesus. What have you learned from God within the last day, week, or month? How can these truths help you in your marriage?

_____

_____

_____

For Your Marriage (choose one or more)

Share today's Straight from God verse with your mate. (Call, text, email, discuss.)

What would you like to learn from Jesus? (Share.) What would your mate like to learn from Jesus? (Ask.)

Share your progress as you learn from Jesus. (Call, text, email, discuss.) Ask God how you can find rest for your soul every day and listen for His response. (Share, discuss.)

NOTES

_____

_____

_____

_____

_____

_____

_____

_____

_____

_____

_____

_____

_____

_____

_____

_____

_____

_____

Week One, Day Three

The Best Thing I Can Do for My Marriage

I'm an introvert and I'm highly-sensitive—which means I don't *have* big feelings, I *am* one big feeling—and I'm a novelist. Which means I could live in my head. Literally, I could spend my days watching the movies and stories in my mind. (Yes, please pray for my husband when you think of him.)

To say I'm list dependent is an understatement. And having too many options, like a plethora of icons on my computer screen, almost makes me break out in hives.

What does any of this have to do with the best thing you can do for your marriage? I'm glad you asked.

Whatever your personality or background, whatever your experience or lack thereof. Your knowledge, education, age, or income. No matter your secret wounds or the private obstacles you face. The best thing you can do for your marriage is standard, timeless, dependable, and guarantees the best return on investment.

Grow your relationship with God.

Continuing with the same text from Ephesians 5:21–33, join me in once again paying careful attention to phrases like "as to the Lord" and "Christ and the church."

Here's the thing. If I want my marriage to be strong. If I want my marriage to thrive. If I want my marriage to last and be loving and caring, and enjoyable and fulfilling and strong. Even in the times I'm irritated or exasperated and feel like I don't care but I wish I cared. The practice that will always produce the results I want is growing my relationship with God.

When I am close to God and have open communication with the Holy Spirit, I'll know what I should and shouldn't do at any given moment. What I should and shouldn't say.

Sometimes it's right to act, but sometimes it's best to be still. Sometimes it's helpful to speak and other times words will only cause strife.

How can I know when to do what? How can I know which way is best?

If I grow my relationship with God, I'll learn to live as God wants me to live. I will learn to live righteously, just like Jesus lived.

And righteousness is always the right answer in marriage.

Righteous behavior is the best behavior for any situation, no matter how big or small. Righteousness is the only standard we need to pursue.

But we can't live righteously without God's help, without His power, provision, and guidance. Which is why you and I must be close to Him. We can't afford not to be. When we aren't close to God, the first human relationship that will suffer is our marriage.

The good news? You can start where you are, no matter what you've done, neglected, or broken.

If you've never started a relationship with God, visit Insight for Living Ministries at https://tinyurl.com/yskhhp2a. Or affirm your relationship with God right now by talking to Him. He longs to help you and teach you everything you need to know. From this day forward, you can choose to make your marriage better than you ever dreamed.

Just for You

Think—reread this week's Scripture passage. God's plan is that your marriage benefits from your walk with Him.

In what way has your relationship with God benefited your marriage or in what way can it benefit your marriage?

_____
_____
_____

Thank God—that as He refines and strengthens you, He is doing the same to your marriage.

In what area of your life is He challenging you to righteousness?

_____
_____
_____

Take—direction from God as He leads you toward righteousness.

What's the first thing God wants you to do to follow righteousness in that specific area?

_____
_____
_____

Straight from God

He restores my soul. He leads me in paths of righteousness for his name's sake. (Psalm 23:3)

This verse mentions being led in paths of righteousness. When has God taught you or changed you step by step? How can that experience encourage you as you walk a new righteous path with God today?

_____
_____
_____

For Your Marriage (choose one or more)

Share today's Straight from God verse with your spouse. (Call, text, email, discuss.)

In what area of your life is God leading you to righteousness? (Share.)

In what area of life is God leading your spouse to righteousness? (Ask.)

Share with each other a time you knew God was leading you on a righteous path. (Call, text, email, discuss.)

Ask God what you can do to help rather than hinder your spouse's spiritual journey and listen for His response. (Share, discuss.)

NOTES

_____

_____

_____

_____

_____

_____

_____

_____

_____

_____

_____

_____

_____

_____

_____

_____

_____

Week One, Day Four

I'm Not a Mind Reader, but I Can Probably Guess the Biggest Problem in Your Marriage

No, I didn't hack into your private email, text messages, or Facebook account. I can barely work our three television remotes. Not kidding.

Still, without seeing you, without talking to you or even knowing your name, I can probably guess the biggest problem in your marriage.

It's whatever you haven't yet, or won't, talk about with God.

Remember, we're studying Ephesians 5:21–33 and seeing how our relationship with God has a direct impact on our marriage. This means anything that affects my relationship with God will directly affect my marriage.

Like … the secret habit I have that God occasionally spotlights, and I haven't yet been able to beat. The behavior I know is wrong or immature, and my pastor spoke on last Sunday.

Or the sin God has been actively confronting in me. The weakness He continues to address, showing me Scriptures, leading me to mentors, and puts right in my face.

Or the hurt inside I need to let God heal, because I'm living reacting to it, and my reactions are harming my relationships. Yep— that's it.

The biggest relational problem in my marriage is one I haven't: Tackled with God.

Surrendered to God. Overcome with God's help. Or let God heal.

Think about it … that temper or short fuse you have. Who bears the brunt of it? Probably your mate. And your children.

Or maybe you have a secret addiction. What relationship suffers most because of it? Your marriage. Your family.

What about the childhood wounds you carry that hinder the closeness and intimacy you and your spouse yearn for? The coping mechanisms you acquired from those wounds that cause behaviors you can't seem to stop. Who suffers right alongside you as that part of your marriage remains stunted and weak? Your mate.

Whatever we refuse to talk to God about will negatively affect our marriage. Whatever we refuse to confront with God's help will negatively affect our marriage.

Yet, here's the great news! The power and provision to overcome these is within our reach. We can choose to stop hurting our marriage and start healing, by letting God into every part of our life.

If you're thinking *it's not a big deal* ... Isn't it?

Did Jesus die so you could have a mediocre marriage? Sporadic intimacy? Weak love? Or downright misery and loneliness in a relationship that is supposed to reflect His love for the world?

Jesus already paid for everything we need to have a healthy, fulfilling marriage. It's all there at the foot of the Cross—gifts, *presents* if you will, wrapped and waiting for us to open and receive.

What gift do you need to pick up and open today? Love? Patience? Self-control? Deliverance? Inner healing? Joy? Or simple kindness?

Everything you need is available and waiting. The stacks of gifts are endless, and every package has your name on it.

Just for You

Think—reread this week's Scripture passage. Every righteous act benefits your marriage. Every sin harms your marriage.

Within the last week, how have you seen this statement to be true?

_____

_____

_____

Thank God—for His work in you, always guiding you to righteousness.

What successes have you had this week in your walk with God?

_____

_____

_____

Take—courage that God will always be at work in you.

What work do you wish God would do in you today?

_____

_____

_____

Straight from God

And I am sure of this, that he who began a good work in you will bring it to completion at the day of Jesus Christ. (Philippians 1:6)

This verse mentions God's faithfulness to complete His work in us. What work do you want God to complete in you in the next month or year? How will your life, behavior, outlook, or attitude change when that work is complete?

_____

_____

_____

For Your Marriage (choose one or more)

Share today's Straight from God verse with your mate. (Call, text, email, discuss.)

Regarding the work you want God to do in you, what is the biggest obstacle to letting God complete this work? (Share.)

How would your mate answer this question? (Ask.)

Ask God to show you how to overcome the obstacle hindering you and listen for His response. (Share, discuss.)

NOTES

_____
_____
_____
_____
_____
_____
_____
_____
_____
_____
_____
_____
_____
_____
_____
_____
_____
_____
_____

The Submission Bomb—It Changes Everything

The subject of submission makes many folks uncomfortable. Some people completely avoid it. Like mammograms. Or colonoscopies.

We don't like the implications. We fear what truth might be revealed. We don't want bad news, or limitations, or to be told what our future holds. Add to that the numerous ways the word has been misused through the years, and some believers would prefer to remove the concept from their Bibles.

By now, you've read the passage in Ephesians 5:21–33 several times. Grit your teeth if you must at the mention of submission, but please, *please* bear with me. Contrary to popular (or unpopular) opinion, it's neither a four-letter word, nor does it mean being a doormat or subservient in a negative sense.

Rather, submission is POWER.

Submission—when manifested correctly, when used righteously—changes everything for the better.

Righteous submission in marriage is like a bomb. It obliterates barriers and obstacles, and it creates an environment where all can be made new.

Does that sound strange? Stay with me. *Think* with me.

If being a believer means being made into the image of Christ, and if marriage between believers is a picture of Christ and the Church, then as married believers we have a scriptural mandate to copy Jesus in every circumstance and situation, especially and including the area of submission.

Was Jesus a doormat? Was he subservient in a negative way? Was he stupid? Less a human, less a man? Of course, not.

Jesus was perfect, righteous, and sinless. He said only what the Father told Him to say (John 12:49–50), and He did all the Father showed Him to do (John 5:19). Jesus lived in complete submission to the Father's will, even to the point of death (Philippians 2:8), and His death on the cross bought our salvation and spiritual freedom.

That is power.

Now I ask you: What if Jesus had said no to the Father about anything? What if He'd said, "I agree to become a man, grow up misunderstood and labeled, then become a preacher and teacher, perform miracles and heal the sick … but I'm not going to die for mankind's sins. That's where I draw the line."

Where would you and I be? What hope would there be for any of us?

But Jesus didn't do that. Yes, He *submitted* to the Father's plan, but not in a doormat kind of way. He didn't simply let whatever was going to happen, happen. His attitude wasn't one of "Oh, well, I guess I'm going to be crucified now."

No, Jesus knew why He was here. Jesus knew His purpose and destiny. And here's the Submission Bomb: Jesus put all His human power—His attitude, energy, and effort—behind the Father's will. He worked to do all the Father asked, even when it hurt, even when it cost Him, even when loving, giving, and healing others were the hardest things to do.

How much stress is a person under when the pressure is so great the capillaries beneath the skin break and bleed (Luke 22:44)?

How difficult was taking the time, caring at all, and healing the servant of the high priest while being arrested (Luke 22:51)?

How tough was it to watch Peter pull back, to feel his abandonment?

To be beaten, tortured, abused, mocked, wounded, and accused?

Still, Jesus submitted to the Father's long-term plan. Jesus didn't try to pretend He wasn't there. He didn't escape the horror and pain through television, or social media, or shopping, or binge eating.

He faced it all, felt it all, and gave all He had to obey the Father's instructions even to the point of death. Christ's submission tore through the temple veil, broke death's hold over us, and provided for our salvation.

That's power. That's scriptural submission. When you and I put all we are—our attitude, energy, and effort—when we put everything in us behind God's plan and keep moving toward it no matter the cost, we create an environment where God can do the impossible.

That's what breaks strongholds within us and breaks down walls within a marriage. When a husband or wife puts everything he or she has behind God's plan and is determined to see it through whatever the cost, miracles can happen.

Love replaces animosity. Joy replaces complacency.

Passion replaces indifference. Stability replaces fear.

I'd planned to challenge or dare you to embrace this perspective. But my burden for your home, for your marriage is so great—instead, I beg you. Study Jesus. Look at His submission to the Father through this filter and ask God how applying this truth can strengthen and unify your marriage.

There's power in submission. Power you can use to conquer every weapon coming against your marriage. Problems, barriers, whatever the issue, use the Submission Bomb to blow them up!

Just for You

Think—reread this week's Scripture passage. Submission to God and His work is one of your greatest spiritual weapons.

What beliefs about submission have hindered you from using this weapon?

_____

_____

_____

Thank God—for Jesus' example of submission and strength.

What behaviors of Jesus show submission combined with strength?

_____

_____

_____

Take—peace from God in the knowledge every difficult-yet-righteous thing He asks you to do will benefit both your relationship with Him and your marriage.

What area of your marriage (expectations, demands, plans, etc.) do you need to submit to God right now?

_____

_____

_____

Straight from God

And being found in human form, he humbled himself by becoming obedient to the point of death, even death on a cross. (Philippians 2:8)

This verse mentions Jesus being obedient to the point of death. What habits, beliefs, or attitudes are prohibiting you from being obedient? How can you submit those habits, beliefs, and attitudes to God?

_____

_____

_____

For Your Marriage (choose one or more)

Share today's Straight from God verse with your spouse. (Call, text, email, discuss.)

What is one area you haven't submitted to God? What are the current personal consequences of your unwillingness? (Confess, share.)

What is one area your spouse hasn't submitted to God? What are the current personal consequences of their unwillingness to submit to God? (Ask, share.)

If submission has been a difficult topic in your marriage, consider and discuss adopting the definition stated in today's reading. (Pray.)

Ask God to reveal any resistance you have to godly submission and listen for His response. (Share, discuss.)

NOTES

_____

_____

_____

_____

_____

_____

_____

_____

_____

_____

_____

_____

_____

_____

_____

Quick Connection for the Weekend

Impact

Which topic from this week affected you the most? Why?

Your marriage as a witnessing tool   Sin as a hindrance
The value of righteousness   The power of submission
Jesus as your example

_____

_____

_____

Deeper Connection

What part of Ephesians 5:21–33 do you find most encouraging?

_____

_____

_____

How can this truth help you grow in God and in your marriage?

_____

_____

_____

What part of Ephesians 5:21–33 do you find most challenging?

_____

_____

_____

What do you need from God to meet this challenge?

_____

_____

_____

In verse 32, Paul uses the word "mystery" regarding marriage, and Christ and the Church. What parts of God do you find most mysterious? Why?

_____

_____

_____

Discuss how your spiritual growth or lack thereof helps/hinders your marriage.

_____

_____

_____

Spiritual growth takes honesty, humility, and effort. Is it time for you to confess an error? Repent of sin? Get help for hurts you brought to the marriage? Seek counseling to learn new skills?

Carry it Forward

How can your spouse help you meet this week's greatest challenge?

_____

_____

_____

How can you help your spouse with this week's greatest challenge?

_____

_____

_____

Pray Together:

Heavenly Father, Thank You for your word that leads us to righteousness. Thank You for the Holy Spirit who teaches us to follow You. We submit to all You are doing in our lives and marriage. Help us love You and each other more each day. In Jesus' name. Amen.

BAD IDEAS

Scriptures for this Week (John 15:1–17)

"¹I am the true vine, and my Father is the vinedresser. ² Every branch in me that does not bear fruit he takes away, and every branch that does bear fruit he prunes, that it may bear more fruit. ³ Already you are clean because of the word that I have spoken to you. ⁴ Abide in me, and I in you. As the branch cannot bear fruit by itself, unless it abides in the vine, neither can you, unless you abide in me.⁵ I am the vine; you are the branches. Whoever abides in me and I in him, he it is that bears much fruit, for apart from me you can do nothing. ⁶ If anyone does not abide in me he is thrown away like a branch and withers; and the branches are gathered, thrown into the fire, and burned. ⁷ If you abide in me, and my words abide in you, ask whatever you wish, and it will be done for you. ⁸ By this my Father is glorified, that you bear much fruit and so prove to be my disciples. ⁹ As the Father has loved me, so have I loved you. Abide in my love. ¹⁰ If you keep my commandments, you will abide in my love, just as I have kept my Father's commandments and abide in his love. ¹¹ These things I have spoken to you, that my joy may be in you, and that your joy may be full. ¹² This is my commandment, that you love one another as I have loved you.¹³ Greater love has no one than this, that someone lay down his life for his friends.¹⁴ You are my friends if you do what I command you. ¹⁵ No longer do I call you servants, for the servant does not know what his master is doing; but I have called you friends, for all that I have heard from my Father I have made known to you. ¹⁶ You did not choose me, but I chose you and appointed you that you should go and bear fruit and that your fruit should abide, so that whatever you ask the Father in my name, he may give it to you. ¹⁷ These things I command you, so that you will love one another."

"Before I Give All of My Heart, He Has to Prove Himself to Me."

I once spoke with a young bride whose parents had encouraged her to view the first years of marriage as the time her husband should prove himself to her. If at the end of five years she wasn't happy, she could simply divorce him. Following their advice, she'd let her groom know he had five years to provide certain things for her—a nice car, a nice home, a particular level of income.

The worst part was, she'd decided to hold back part of her heart.

She'd gotten a job, and she was keeping that income separate, saving up in case her husband and her marriage failed.

This young bride was not fully invested in her marriage. And her marriage suffered greatly because of her choices. She and her husband had affairs even after they had children. Even after they'd gotten involved in a good church. She was always looking for a better opportunity, a better life, rather than building a life with her husband.

I must admit, at times I still see myself in that young woman. Even though I've been married for over thirty-seven years and have never had an affair, I still discover parts of myself I've withheld from my husband. Sometimes with intent, but usually without me realizing.

The revelation of parts of me I haven't shared always comes in direct response to God's work in me. When He convicts me to repent—change my mind and my actions by turning away from harmful actions and embracing God's directions about how to live my life—inevitably He prompts me to apologize to my husband for how that behavior has affected him and my marriage. I open that part of me through repentance.

Sometimes God teaches me something new and impresses me to share that with my husband. I open myself through discovery and sharing of knowledge.

Sometimes God heals something in me and pushes me to let my husband know what's happened, especially if we've prayed together about that particular hurt. I open myself through healing.

Opening all of myself to my husband is what completes the circuit between us and establishes new growth in my marriage.

In Matthew 19:16–30, we see the story of the rich young ruler. This young man asks Jesus how he can have eternal life. He assures Jesus he keeps all the commandments—an obvious impossibility, no one other than Jesus is perfect.

Yet Jesus treats the young man as if he's telling the truth. As if he is indeed a perfect Jew, keeping all the commandments. Then the conversation continues. Verses twenty-one and twenty-two show us one of the saddest scenes in Scripture.

"Jesus said to him, 'If you would be perfect, go, sell what you possess and give to the poor, and you will have treasure in heaven; and come, follow me.' When the young man heard this he went away sorrowful, for he had great possessions" (Matthew 19:21–22).

The young man wasn't willing to give up what was most important to him. An obvious idol in his life, his wealth. One big, big thing between him and God.

Whatever we withhold might be the one thing we most need to give or offer in our marriage. It might be the one piece that's keeping everything else from falling into place.

Are you all in? Are you giving all, giving everything to your marriage?

If not, what are you withholding? And why?

Give all. Depend on God. And watch your marriage and your love grow.

Just for You

Think—reread this week's Scripture passage. You are God's first priority.

How does God demonstrate you're His first priority?

_____

_____

_____

Thank God—He knows everything about you, even the hurts, dreams, and requests you find hard to put into words.

What do you find most difficult to pray about—hurts, dreams, or requests? Why?

_____

_____

_____

Take—comfort in the knowledge you don't have to explain every little thing to God, yet He is willing to talk and listen at every moment.

What one thing do you most need to talk about with Him?

_____

_____

_____

Straight from God

"Why, even the hairs of your head are all numbered. Fear not; you are of more value than many sparrows." (Luke 12:7)

This statement from Jesus shows God values you. You have worth to Him and He loves you. Are you withholding anything from your relationship with Him? Write a short prayer giving that part of yourself to Him. "Heavenly Father, I give you _____."

_____

_____

_____

For Your Marriage (choose one or more)

Share today's Straight from God verse with your spouse. (Call, text, email, discuss.)

What do you find most difficult to give your mate? (Confess, share.)

How badly does your mate need that from you? (Ask.)

What does your mate find most difficult to give to you? (Ask.)

How badly do you need that from your spouse? (Share.)

Give the most difficult part of your marriage to God in prayer. (Share, discuss, pray.)

Ask God to help you understand how much He values you and your marriage and listen for His response. (Share, discuss.)

NOTES

_____
_____
_____
_____
_____
_____
_____
_____
_____
_____
_____
_____
_____
_____
_____
_____
_____

Week Two, Day Two

"The One Who's Wrong Is the One Who Must Change."

I admit. I love being right.

And the longer I live the more I realize I've been wrong about many things. The desire to be right can be a symptom of fear, pride, uncertainty, or even a desire to please. It can become an obsession, and it can back us into a corner—a lonely, isolated corner.

Years ago, a young lady I knew was considering marriage. During a conversation, she expressed concern about a particular topic she and her fiancé disagreed about. She was convinced she was right, and I could tell she was very afraid of being wrong or being told she was wrong.

"Which one of us has to change?" she asked.

I understood her concerns. And I saw the challenge in her eyes, daring me to pick one over the other.

"Both of you," I said. "If you're going to do marriage God's way, both of you will have to change again and again for the rest of your lives."

That wasn't the answer she wanted to hear. Eventually, the engagement ended, because she insisted she was right in her opposition to a concept clearly endorsed in Scripture.

If you've ever broken or sprained a limb, you know what it's like to have to compensate for a weakness. Your whole body must work to accommodate one part that isn't working properly. When the break or sprain is healed, the muscles that adjusted to the weakness must readjust to work properly. Once again, you're sore all over.

The same phenomenon happens in marriage. When there's a weakness, the other parts of the relationship must compensate. When that weakness is rectified, every part of the relationship must readjust.

While that adjustment period can be uncomfortable, if we refuse to adjust our marriage will suffer.

Which means in my marriage, even if only one of us is wrong, or clueless, or careless—once that discrepancy is resolved both of us must change. Every time one of us grows spiritually, we need to make adjustments. Every time one of us matures and every time one of us creates a new, good habit. Otherwise, we never experience all the fruit of that growth.

We've all seen couples who survive a tough trial, then the marriage ends because they didn't readjust after the crisis. We've all seen marriages end in divorce, then it seems one party's new spouse reaps the benefits of all the growth process in that person, after the first spouse endured all the struggle.

In 2 Corinthians 3:18 we read, "And we all, with unveiled face, beholding the glory of the Lord, are being transformed into the same image from one degree of glory to another. For this comes from the Lord who is the Spirit."

As we walk with God, we are changed. As we walk in marriage together, we must change.

What area of your life needs to change? What negative impact is that weakness currently having on your marriage?

Seek spiritual growth. Seek change. Then, readjust and encourage your beloved to do the same. That way, you'll both reap the benefits of your transformations.

Just for You

Think—reread this week's Scripture passage. God wants to transform you by His Spirit.

What areas of your life has God already changed for the better?

_____

_____

_____

Thank God—for these changes.

What area of your life would you like Him to change next?

_____

_____

_____

Take—instruction from God regarding this area.

What is God telling you about this area of your life?

_____

_____

_____

Straight from God

But grow in the grace and knowledge of our Lord and Savior Jesus Christ. To him be the glory both now and to the day of eternity. Amen. (2 Peter 3:18)

As we grow in God, He changes us for the better. When God changes the area of your life you wrote above, what glory will it bring to Him?

_____

_____

_____

For Your Marriage (choose one or more)

Share today's Straight from God verse with your mate. (Call, text, email, discuss.)

How has your marriage benefited from areas you've let God change in you? (Share, discuss.)

How has your marriage benefited from areas your spouse has let God change in them? (Ask, share, discuss.)

How do these positive changes manifest God's work and glory? (Ask, share, discuss, pray.)

Ask God to help you recognize opportunities to share His glory with others and listen for His response. (Share, discuss.)

NOTES

_____

_____

_____

_____

_____

_____

_____

_____

_____

_____

_____

_____

_____

_____

_____

Week Two, Day Three

"Wives, Stop Expecting Your Husbands to Hear from God."

I'm not making this up. When I heard this statement, I was certain I'd misunderstood.

The speaker is a prominent Christian teacher on marriage. When I heard him say these words, "Wives, stop expecting your husbands to hear from God," his television show aired on two different stations at two different times in my area, so I purposely waited and watched a second time to be sure I'd accurately heard him.

Yep. I'd heard him right.

His explanation went something like this. In his years of counseling Christian couples, he was appalled and concerned at the number of women who were frustrated with their husbands for not having open communication with God, especially concerning important decisions or family issues.

His relief for this frustration was simple. Wives shouldn't expect their husbands to hear from God. Rather, wives should be the primary listeners to God then tell their husbands what God said. Husbands can then implement whatever God said. "Wives, you'll be happier," this teacher said. "The tension in the marriage will melt away."

I was dumbfounded. And I was angry.

Angry on behalf of every wife who'd taken his advice and short circuited and devalued her husband's spiritual growth.

Angry on behalf of every husband whose wife would expect him to forfeit his own spiritual journey. Every husband who might actually use this horrible idea as an excuse to leave hearing God to his wife and exempt himself from a growing intimacy with God.

It's one thing to remind wives of their need to hear from God. It's another to negate a husband's need to hear God.

In reality, the spiritual condition of my marriage is dependent on both me and my husband interacting with God, listening to Him, and following Him. To do marriage God's way, both of us must be in an active and growing relationship with God, then mimic His love and behavior in everything we do.

I'll be honest with you. At times my husband and I have failed miserably. There have been strongholds in my husband's life I thought he'd never talk to God about, let alone overcome. There have been seasons I was so disillusioned or disappointed with God, times when I was so wrong about Him, I told Stephen, "Don't even pray for me."

There have even been times when bad habits and wounds and coping mechanisms from stuff we went through when we were younger left us with little to no spiritual connection with each other, and neither of us was talking with God except to complain about the other.

I understand how frustrating it can be to wait on your mate to get on the same page you are spiritually. I get how disheartened a person can feel when it seems their mate doesn't engage spiritually or downright resists seeking spiritual growth.

Yet, the answer to frustration with my husband (when we're not on the same page spiritually) isn't negating or derailing his spiritual journey. The solution isn't me taking over, so I can control what's happening. Or leaving my husband behind.

The righteous choice is for me to love Stephen like Jesus loves me, even if that means I don't get a solution to a problem right away. Sometimes it means loving my husband through his season of learning and letting God do a work in him, without me making demands or insisting my expectations are met.

The bottom line many of us don't want to admit is God's priorities are different from ours. He's much more concerned with the depth of our relationship with Him than He is with our completing tasks. He cares more about how we treat each other while we grow, when we disagree, and during the times we don't get what we want, than about making our lives easy.

He uses pressure to prune us. He uses inconvenience and frustration to provoke us to prayer and dependence on Him.

When the spiritual balance in my marriage is uneven, He is calling me to greater intimacy with Him. To abide with fervor and listen. Because today my mate might be struggling spiritually, but tomorrow, it could be me.

Just for You

Think—reread this week's Scripture passage. Hearing from God is important when making decisions, during a crisis, and in everyday life.

How do you discern God's voice?

_____

_____

_____

Thank God—for all the answers and wisdom He has already given you.

Describe a time God gave you wisdom and direction.

_____

_____

_____

Take—peace in the knowledge God always has every answer you need.

What wisdom and direction do you need from Him now?

_____

_____

_____

Straight from God

"But the Helper, the Holy Spirit, whom the Father will send in my name, he will teach you all things and bring to your remembrance all that I have said to you." (John 14:26)

Jesus promised the Holy Spirit would teach us and help us remember what we learn. What is one truth you learned about God in the past? How can that truth help you now?

_____

_____

_____

For Your Marriage (choose one or more)

Share today's Straight from God verse with your mate. (Call, text, email, discuss.)

What do you need God to teach you right now to strengthen your marriage? (Share.)

What do you want your spouse to ask God to teach them to strengthen your marriage? (Share.)

Which is most difficult for you—showing love to, showing appreciation for, giving honor to, or cherishing your mate? Why? (Share, ask, discuss.)

Ask God to teach you how to overcome this weakness and listen for His response. (Share, discuss.)

NOTES

_____

_____

_____

_____

_____

_____

_____

_____

_____

_____

_____

_____

Week Two, Day Four

"Are You Unhappy? Maybe You'll Be Happier Separated."

Building a healthy marriage is work. Hard work—on ourselves.

My husband and I had so much stacked against us when we married. We brought more baggage than—well, I don't know what, but trust me, we brought truckloads. Even though we'd dated for three and a half years and were friends before that, we'd only scratched the surface of learning each other. And neither of us had any idea of the colossal messes and piles of trash inside ourselves.

We've had seasons when the same problem surfaced almost every day, year after year. We've had seasons when almost everything I said to him hit him the wrong way, or vice versa. We've had times when I've wondered if I made the biggest mistake of my life marrying him, and no doubt, he's wondered the same.

There have been moments when we've looked at each other and it seemed love, forgiveness, kindness, or favor for the other were so far away we'd never again find them.

I admit that more than once, I've lain awake in the middle of the night wondering how much easier my life might be if we weren't married. I know there have been times Stephen felt the same.

I was tired of the same old problems. Or flattened by a new one that seemed unbeatable. At times, I just wanted relief and separation looked like a shiny diamond of an option.

Unfortunately, most people, including believers, misuse separation. They feel lighter at the absence of conflict, and think they've finally found the paradise they long for complete with greener grass, rainbows, and happy unicorns.

However, Scripture shows us separation is not a trial period to see if I'm happier living apart from my husband. It's not an opportunity to see if I can survive, financially, or otherwise, without my mate.

Rather, according to 1 Corinthians 7:5, separation is a time when I am to devote myself to prayer and fasting. It's supposed to be a concentrated time of me listening to God, to hear what He has to say about my life and my marriage.

"Do not deprive one another, except perhaps by agreement for a limited time, that you may devote yourselves to prayer; but then come together again, so that Satan may not tempt you because of your lack of self-control" (1 Corinthians 7:5).

True, no matter how hard you pray you can't make someone stay or do the right thing. If your spouse wants to walk away permanently in blatant disobedience to God, you can't stop them. But as far as it concerns you, as for your part, you can choose to handle any separation biblically. Which means separating yourself *to* God more than separating yourself *from* your mate.

Is any area of your marriage in crisis? Do you wish you could turn back time and not marry your spouse? Is there so much tension in your home you grab any excuse to leave the house—a quick trip to the grocery store or an awful trip to the dentist? Please find a source of sound, scriptural counseling. Still, good counsel won't help unless you separate yourself to God.

Put more time into prayer than you would in an attorney's office.

More time than you'd spend shuffling your children back and forth for weekend visits.

More time than you've spent daydreaming about divorce and what your new life could be.

Most importantly, fast. Set aside the many things you've used to soothe yourself. Set aside digital devices, social media, your best friend, or church groups if they serve only to distract you. Even chocolate if you tend to use it for comfort rather than depending on God.

Get face-to-face with God. Concentrate on Him, only on Him, until you have answers, strength, grace, and provision to move forward as He wills. Ask Him to put love where there is no love. Ask Him to put joy where there is no joy.

I know—I've lived it, I'm living it still—if both parties listen to and obey God, He can redeem, heal, and make new any marriage.

With God's help, you can live happily *even* after—harsh words, deep hurts, or terrible mistakes. God can give beauty for ashes. If any area of your marriage is a heap of rubble, give Him your full attention, so He can work a miracle.

Just for You

Think—reread this week's Scripture passage. Jesus often went away to pray to spend time alone with His Father, address His own needs, and fortify Himself for all of life's demands.

Do you need concentrated prayer time, either about your relationship with Him or your marriage? How can you set aside more time for just you and God?

_____

_____

_____

Thank God—for the power of prayer and fasting.

What can you fast from today or this week as a sacrifice to God and in request of His wisdom?

_____

_____

_____

Take—time to focus on all God wants to give you in your marriage, all He wants to teach you and prove to you through your marriage.

What is one difficult or negative thing in your marriage you'd like God to replace with something beautiful and good?

_____

_____

_____

Straight from God

Anyone who does not love does not know God, because God is love. (1 John 4:8)

God *is* love. This means when God puts love in our heart for our mate, He's given us part of His character and presence. So, learning more about God will cause our love to grow even if our mate and marriage are imperfect. In what area of your marriage do you need a special dispensation of His character and presence? In what area of your marriage have you seen the miraculous effects of God's presence and love?

_____

_____

_____

For Your Marriage (choose one or more)

Share today's Straight from God verse with your beloved. (Call, text, email, discuss.)

If there's a reason you have considered separation, that's exactly the area God where wants to work a miracle. Talk with Him about that area and listen to His response, then share with your mate what God said to you. (Call, text, email, discuss.)

Give your mate the opportunity to do the same. (Ask, share, discuss.)

When have you seen the power of God's love in action? (Share.)

When has your mate loved you with God's supernatural love? (Thank them.)

What supernatural love do you need from your mate now? (Ask.)

Ask God to teach you something new about showing love to your mate and listen for His response. (Share, discuss.)

NOTES

_____

_____

_____

_____

_____

_____

_____

_____

_____

_____

_____

Week Two, Day Five

"Go Ahead and Get a Divorce. Kids Are Resilient."

I know a pastor who actually told a young mother if she sought divorce, her child would be fine. "Kids are resilient," he said. "Your daughter will be fine."

The wife had no biblical grounds for a divorce, she was simply unhappy. There were reasons for that unhappiness, but none were critical or came from blatant sinful behavior by her husband. Unfortunately, the pastor either wasn't aware of or didn't consider the long-term effects divorce can have on children.

As a child from a broken home, I was twice as likely to drop out of school as someone from an intact home. Three times as likely to have a baby out of wedlock. Five times more likely to be in poverty, and twelve times more likely to end up incarcerated.

I have a greater than seventy-five percent chance of getting divorced than someone whose parents are still married to each other, which means a less than twenty-five percent chance that a marriage I'm part of will actually work. This is according to Judith S. Wallerstein, Julia M. Lewis, and Sandra Blakeslee's *The Unexpected Legacy of Divorce*: *The Twenty-five Year Landmark Study*, which followed one hundred children of divorce for twenty-five years after parental divorce, as documented in Bridget E. Maher's, "The Benefits of Marriage" (2005). As you can see, these statistics are almost twenty years old, and have obviously worsened since this study was done.

I'm five times more likely to suffer from mental problems. If you ask my husband at the right time of the month, he might tell you that's definitely true!

Some people say, "But kids cope. They adapt."

Not exactly. The truth is they survive. They don't have the vocabulary or the skills to cope without consequences. They compartmentalize, repress, or suppress. They become adults with problems rooted in the divorce.

"But we're so unhappy, it can't be healthy for my children to live with unhappy parents," some say.

If Scripture allows and God is telling you to end the marriage, be 110 percent sure that's what He's telling you and be obedient. But if you're simply unhappy, even if you're really unhappy, there's more to consider.

Rather than seeking divorce because of unhappiness, or because I don't feel in love with my mate today, or my marriage is all but dead and we haven't even spoken to each other in days, or I just want to start over with someone else—I can choose to ask God to do a work. Even if it's a long-term work. I can choose to model a life God is actively renovating, a marriage He turns into a miracle.

For those who endured divorce but didn't seek it (your spouse sought it), I encourage you to heal from those wounds and help your children do the same. It will be a tough road, but with God's help you can do it.

If you sought an unrighteous divorce and now regret it, I encourage you to help your children heal. It'll be tough. You'll have to own up to your mistakes.

If you're now at a crossroads weighing the pros and cons of getting a divorce but don't have scriptural grounds, please stay and seek to fix the marriage. Scripture allows for divorce when there's adultery, abuse, your mate chooses to live as an unbeliever, or if your mate leaves the marriage. You can't choose how your spouse behaves, but as for you, do all God requires to heal the marriage.

I'm not trying to sound insensitive or harsh. I'm sharing with you the harsh realities of living as a child, then an adult, from a broken home. Even when divorcing parents are civil to each other, the child of divorce suffers the consequences throughout his or her adult life. Google "problems children of divorce have in adult life" if you need a reason to try again.

As a growing believer, I am continually learning to recognize my own sin, as well as every person's need for God, including my children and family. Their greatest need is to know God and believe He will work in their lives.

The best thing for our children is giving them the opportunity to watch God fix an unhealthy marriage. This will benefit them more than getting a divorce, because one day they will probably marry and face struggles of their own.

If you can choose to build a healthy marriage—even if it requires a lot of work—I promise you would choose that for your children over the on-going challenges children of divorce face. Your children's future and your testimony are worth the effort.

Just for You

Think—reread this week's Scripture passage. All your decisions affect you and others.

How did Jesus's decisions affect those around Him?

_____

_____

_____

Thank God—you don't have to make decisions alone.

What decision weighs most heavily on you right now?

_____

_____

_____

Take—the burden of decision, and the feeling of control that goes with it, and give both to God.

What stops you from being obedient to God?

_____

_____

_____

Straight from God

If any of you lacks wisdom, let him ask God, who gives generously to all without reproach, and it will be given him. (James 1:5)

God is very generous when giving wisdom. He knows more about my heart and motivations than I do. He knows more about my beloved's heart and motivations than I do. When we ask God for wisdom and listen for His direction, He will show us what to do and how to do it, both in simple things and tough things. What simple and tough things is God asking you to do now?

_____

_____

_____

For Your Marriage (choose one or more)

Share today's Straight from God verse with your beloved. (Call, text, email, discuss.)

What wisdom do you need in your marriage right now? (Share.)

What wisdom does your spouse need right now? (Ask.)

Ask God to give you wisdom about a small problem and a larger problem, then listen for His response. (Share, discuss.)

NOTES

_____

_____

_____

_____

_____

_____

_____

_____

_____

_____

_____

_____

_____

_____

_____

_____

_____

_____

_____

_____

Quick Connection for the Weekend

Impact

Which topic from this week affected you the most? Why?

Before I give all of me   Maybe you'll be happier separated
The one who's wrong must change   Kids are resilient
Wives, stop expecting your husbands to hear from God

Deeper Connection
What part of John 15:1–17 do you find most encouraging?

How can this truth help you grow in God and in your marriage?

What part of John 15:1–17 do you find most challenging?

What do you need from God to meet this challenge?

In verse 4, Jesus uses the word "abide" eleven times in this passage regarding our relationship with Him. What does it look like to abide with God and in God?

_____

_____

_____

Being "all in," being changed into Christ's image, hearing God, becoming one with your mate, and having a healthy marriage all start at the same place—a growing relationship with God. We cannot successfully abide with each other if we don't abide with Him. Within the past week, when have you been successful and unsuccessful at abiding in God and with your spouse?

_____

_____

_____

In John 15, Jesus directly connects remaining in His love with the command to love each other. Describe a time you knew you didn't show love in your marriage and how that affected your spiritual life. Describe a time you knew you did show love in your marriage and how that affected your spiritual life.

_____

_____

_____

Carry it Forward

What is one thing you need from your beloved to help you meet this week's greatest challenge?

_____

_____

_____

What is one thing you can do for your beloved to help him with this week's greatest challenge?

_____

_____

_____

Pray together:

Heavenly Father, Thank You that when we abide in You we have access to wisdom and guidance for our lives. Thank You for growing us to be more like You. Help us find joy in loving You and each other. In Jesus's name. Amen.

COMFORT

Scriptures for This Week (Psalm 46)

[1]God is our refuge and strength, a very present help in trouble. [2] Therefore we will not fear though the earth gives way, though the mountains be moved into the heart of the sea, [3] though its waters roar and foam, though the mountains tremble at its swelling. Selah [4] There is a river whose streams make glad the city of God, the holy habitation of the Most High. [5] God is in the midst of her; she shall not be moved; God will help her when morning dawns. [6] The nations rage, the kingdoms totter; he utters his voice, the earth melts. [7]The Lord of hosts is with us; the God of Jacob is our fortress. Selah [8] Come, behold the works of the Lord, how he has brought desolations on the earth. [9] He makes wars cease to the end of the earth; he breaks the bow and shatters the spear; he burns the chariots with fire. [10] "Be still, and know that I am God. I will be exalted among the nations, I will be exalted in the earth!" [11] The Lord of hosts is with us; the God of Jacob is our fortress. Selah

The Valentine's Day That Wasn't

Valentine's Day and other holidays are accompanied by a lot of pressure and expectation, especially in regard to marriage. Days like these can be full of turmoil and disappointment. They're not always the romantic, harmonious events we'd prefer. Rather, they can leave us hurting.

The absence of a card or gift, or the presence of a particular card or gift can symbolize your marriage is on shaky ground or sliding toward a dangerous precipice. Maybe it's already fallen over the cliff. Maybe it's already shattered.

If your special occasion or Valentine's Day *wasn't*, I'm sorry. I really am. You might be hurting, or worse, numb. Either way, my heart aches for you and your spouse.

God's heart aches, as well.

I pray what I'm about to say will give you hope when any disappointment comes no matter the date or day. I pray what I'm about to say will strengthen you and assure you you're not alone facing whatever is threatening your marriage.

The condition of your marriage isn't a surprise to God.

God knows the factors contributing to the condition of your marriage. God knows how to fix your marriage. He's not only *able*, He's *available*.

Rest in that today. Don't try to do anything or change anything, unless God tells you specifically to do so. Just … rest.

Rest in the knowledge God is not only powerful, He is prepared.

Rest in the fact Jesus already paid the price for your sin, and for the consequences of other people's sin on both you and your mate.

Rest in the assurance you don't have to face one moment, not a millionth of a second alone.

God is present. Amidst the rubble and mess, He is there.

Sit with Him. Let Him hold you. Hide your face against His shoulder if you want to. Weep there if you need to.

Whatever you do, don't move until He tells you to. Simply stay there and rest.

Just for You

Think—reread this week's Scripture passage. No matter what threatens your marriage, God is your personal refuge.

When has God helped you in previous times of trouble?

_____

_____

_____

Thank God—you don't have to face trouble alone.

What trouble within or outside your marriage are you facing now?

_____

_____

_____

Take—comfort in God's promise to be present in trouble.

What stops you from trusting God to defend and strengthen you?

_____

_____

_____

Straight from God

The name of the Lord is a strong tower; the righteous man runs into it and is safe. (Proverbs 18:10)

Sometimes our world is a very threatening place. When we feel emotionally threatened in our marriage, our first consideration should be God, His character, and all His promises in Scripture. We should run to Him, listen, and obey all He says to do. What commands of God are most difficult to follow when you feel threatened?

_____

_____

_____

For Your Marriage (choose one or more)

Share today's Straight from God verse with your spouse. (Call, text, email, discuss.)

What threatens your marriage today? From within? From without? (Share, discuss.)

What threat have you brought to the marriage you need to repent of? (Confess, share.)

What threat has your spouse brought to the marriage they need to repent of? (Ask, discuss, pray.)

How can you and your mate work together to decrease these threats? (Discuss, pray.)

Ask God to show you when simply running to Him for safety is the best choice and listen for His response. (Share, discuss.)

NOTES

_____
_____
_____
_____
_____
_____
_____
_____
_____
_____
_____
_____
_____

If You Were Given Horrible Advice before You Married

I'll call her Annie. Annie meant well. She really did.

Four days before I married, she had this to say regarding my imminent honeymoon and sex: "I hope you're not disappointed."

That simple statement told me volumes about her opinions and her experience. I responded with a pithy comment that embarrassed her, and the discussion ended.

Obviously, I still remember that conversation. And more than once I've wondered how many others have been given horrifically bad advice right before marriage by those who didn't know better. By those who meant well, but really didn't have anything good to offer. Or by those who offered what they had, but what they had was severely lacking in quality.

Please, please, *please*—if you can't find it in Scripture, question everything you were told about marriage, no matter who said it.

If it doesn't line up with God's character, throw it out.

If it doesn't help you in your walk with God and your walk together toward becoming one, throw it out!

People share truth as they know it. They speak from their ignorance, their wounds, their prejudices and blindness as they peer around the beam in their own eye. Even well-meaning folks, because they're just as imperfect as we are. They're dealing with their trash and still growing in God just like you and me.

Gently setting aside unwise counsel isn't disrespectful. Choosing a different path isn't dishonoring. It's not rebellious to carefully consider input about marriage, or any other topic, and weigh it against Scripture as the believers in Berea did, who were applauded for their pursuit of truth (Acts 17:10–11).

Put aside your loyalty to a person or movement. A person can be sincere and still be sincerely wrong.

Consider the cornerstones of your marriage. If you were asked today to write a mission statement for your relationship with your beloved, would it be scripturally sound? Would you want to pass it on to your children? Would you want them to copy what they see in your marriage?

Examine where you are in your marriage.

Is there an unhealthy part, a dim corner where you've embraced a notion you were taught was "normal," or "standard operating procedure?" Has God's Spirit been gently but consistently tapping you on the shoulder about a particular topic?

Release your marriage from fetters of ignorance and misinformation. Discuss this with God.

Listen. Learn. Change. Grow. And let God's truth help you become one.

Just for You

Think—reread this week's Scripture passage. God is our refuge because He has all the answers and truths we need.

How important is following the truth of Scripture in your life? Why?

_____

_____

_____

Thank God—He is a place to hide, ponder, and receive wisdom.

How do you regularly spend time in God's presence? What can you do to increase the quantity and quality of that time?

_____

_____

_____

Take—conviction and direction from God's Spirit challenging all you've heard from others.

What beliefs do you need to set aside? What truths do you need to more fully embrace?

_____

_____

_____

Straight from God

For the word of God is living and active, sharper than any two-edged sword, piercing to the division of soul and of spirit, of joints and of marrow, and discerning the thoughts and intentions of the heart. (Hebrews 4:12)

God's word can convict, enlighten, teach, and empower us. When we read and meditate on Scripture, we are opening ourselves to God's continued work in us. Through His Word, God will challenge our beliefs, habits, and attitudes. What life-changing truth has God most recently revealed to you? How is that truth changing your walk with Him? How is it changing your marriage?

_____

_____

_____

For Your Marriage (choose one or more)

Share today's Straight from God verse with your mate. (Call, text, email, discuss.)
What are your favorite Scriptures? Why? (Share.)
What are your beloved's favorite Scriptures? Why? (Ask.)
Choose a Scripture to focus on together. (Discuss, pray.)
Ask God to reveal any biblical truths you have avoided and why, then listen for His response. (Share, discuss.)

NOTES

_____
_____
_____
_____
_____
_____
_____
_____
_____
_____
_____
_____
_____
_____
_____
_____
_____
_____

Week Three, Day Three

If You're in a Tough Season or If Your Marriage Simply Isn't Working

Hopefully, my middle son won't hate me for sharing this. It was one of those events that is so cute to parents but also shows the honesty of children.

He was about to turn four, and he knew his birthday was coming. He and his older brother were invited to a birthday party for one of his brother's friends.

We arrived early, as I'd promised to help set up. I figured I'd spend most of my time corralling my youngest, since he was a little too young to play with the bigger kids. By the front door sat a table holding gifts for the birthday boy. My son took one look at the growing pile of presents and asked, "Where are *my* presents?"

I explained it wasn't his turn yet, his birthday was still weeks away.

He was completely offended, as only an almost four-year-old can be, and announced if he didn't get presents, too, he wasn't "doing" the party. He spent the entire afternoon sitting under the table protesting the injustice of it all.

Most people don't get married planning to be unhappy. We have expectations. There's a list in our head of the benefits and perks we think we'll receive simply because we're doing the marriage thing.

And you know what? We should have expectations. The breath God breathed into us, the fact we are made in God's image, means we were built for relationship. We long for it. Our need for intimacy is a deep need.

Dissatisfaction, unhappiness, and disappointment are simply indicators we haven't quite reached the intimacy we long for. The good news is there's hope for the husband and wife who want more.

A closer marriage, a stronger union is within reach for the husband and wife who will do marriage God's way.

But how do I do that, you ask? *Where do I start?*

I've made this suggestion to many couples. The ones who have diligently tried it and stuck to it have reaped more benefits than they sought.

Tithe your marriage.

I'm not talking about dollars or placing value on specific aspects of your marriage. I mean based on how long you've been married, place a tithe of that before God, giving Him time to do a new work.

So, if you've been married five years, that's sixty months. Together—or if your spouse is resistant, do it yourself—set aside the next six months to do nothing but seek God. Lay down your expectations about your marriage at Jesus's feet. Lay down your hurts, wounds, or disappointments. Lay down your pride or desire to pronounce judgment on another. Lay down your will.

Approach this season with an attitude of sacrifice to God. Don't try or seek to change your marriage; simply focus on your relationship with God.

Give this time to God to do whatever work He chooses in you.

I don't mean ignore or neglect your mate. Rather, during this time love as God loves, because that's what He calls us to do. Give as God gives, again, because that's what He calls us to do. Spend time seeking to cultivate the Fruit of the Spirit (Galatians 5), embrace and exemplify the Beatitudes (Matthew 5), and carve 1 Corinthians 13 on your heart.

Simply set apart this period of time for deep spiritual growth and renewal. Plant the time in new soil, water and nurture it without baggage or blame, and let God produce the fruit.

By doing this, you will know you have invested all, given all, because you've let God work in you to benefit your walk with Him and your marriage. No matter what happens, you will never regret this season.

Why wait? Try it for a month. Thirty days of intense and purposeful spiritual growth. Thirty days isn't a lot to ask, especially if it saves you, your mate, and your children from decades of heartache.

Just for You

Think—reread this week's Scripture passage. How you spend your time affects every area of your life.

Why do you think Jesus spent so much time in prayer?

_____

_____

_____

Thank God—that no investment in your relationship with Him is wasted.

When have you made a sacrificial gift to someone (time, money, etc.)?

_____

_____

_____

Take—encouragement that if God places a difficult task before you, He will equip you to do that task.

If you tithed your marriage beginning today, what fruit would you want God to grow in you and your marriage?

_____

_____

_____

Straight from God

Then he ordered the crowds to sit down on the grass, and taking the five loaves and the two fish, he looked up to heaven and said a blessing. Then he broke the loaves and gave them to the disciples, and the disciples gave them to the crowds. (Matthew 14:19)

When we give to God, even in our lack, God can multiply our efforts. He will bless that gift, then He will break it. Consider a time when

God has healed brokenness in you. What did you learn from that experience? How can you apply those truths to any area of brokenness in your life or marriage today?

_____

_____

_____

For Your Marriage (choose one or more)

Share today's Straight from God verse with your spouse. (Call, text, email, discuss.)

What is God asking you to offer Him today? (Share.)

What is God asking your mate to offer Him today? (Ask.)

Discuss a time you (as individuals or together) didn't sacrifice something God had told you to. What were the consequences? (Discuss, confess, pray.)

Ask God to reveal hidden areas of brokenness in your life or marriage and listen for His response. (Share, discuss.)

NOTES

_____

_____

_____

_____

_____

_____

_____

_____

_____

_____

_____

_____

_____

_____

Are You Divorced Inside?

The Chinese philosopher Lao-tzu is credited with the classic quotation, "A journey of a thousand miles begins with a single step." So it is with separation, affairs, divorce, and every other choice that threatens the health of any marriage—someone takes a first step.

Every moment, you and I choose to love or not, talk or not, reach for and be held or not, stay or not. Not one marriage falls apart without one or both parties taking steps to end it. A foreign entity cannot file for divorce on my behalf. I can't have an affair by proxy.

One speaker and writer on marriage (whom I won't name) encourages readers in his book that "sticking it out" in marriage is a victory. He says staying married is a testimony in itself.

I totally, completely disagree. If I stay married simply so I don't get divorced, how does that bring glory to God? If a couple stays married on the outside for the sake of appearance, but they aren't kind to each other, don't love each other, have no joy in each other, and their union is a pitiful demonstration of God's love and power, of Christ's commitment and sacrifice for His bride, what glory for God is in that?

Many times, I've been tempted to stop trying, stop reaching for my husband, and let distance between us grow. The idea of giving up was so appealing. I was tired of trying to connect and reach real unity, especially in the shadowy spaces of my marriage where the probability of conflict was high.

But God convicted me of wishing I could pick and choose which areas of my marriage would have true intimacy and which areas would be nothing but a façade. Even though I wasn't choosing to legally seek a visible divorce, I realized maintaining the illusion of a Christian marriage while fostering a divorced mentality in my heart was hypocrisy in its purest form.

My kids would see it. My friends would see it. Unbelievers would see it. And I would be living a lie.

If you're divorced inside—in a small way or a big way—first know that I'm sorry. I know that area hurts you. Maybe you're way past hurting over the condition of your marriage.

When did this distance appear? After ten years of marriage? Five years? Five days?

Maybe you thought marriage would be easy. Maybe you thought your marriage would be different than others you've seen. Maybe you thought your mate was stronger in certain areas, had better self-control, and would never, ever fail and hurt you as you've been hurt.

Well, it just happened, you say. *We grew apart. We fell out of love.*

Is that really the truth? You took steps toward each other before, then at some point, you stopped. The question is, why?

Let me encourage you. There is no limit to the healing and strength God can bring to your marriage, just as there's no limit to the healing and strength God can bring to your individual lives.

It's that simple. It's not easy, but it is simple.

Choosing to walk back to our mate is an act of will that often requires the Holy Spirit's power. Choosing to reopen our heart can be even more difficult. Learning to choose to cultivate love, let God change us, and grow us into all He wants us to be, is a true act of submission to God.

If we let a mentality of divorce reign in an area of our heart, haven't we basically told God we have the right to withhold that area of our heart from our mate?

No matter how your marriage began, no matter the broken condition of some areas of your marriage, God can still redeem it. God can start right now, right where you are today. Ask Him to bring unity, harmony, life, and growth where death and decay reign.

Just for You

Think—reread this week's Scripture passage. God places high priority on protecting and preserving a healthy marriage.

What areas of your marriage are healthy and functioning well?

_____

_____

_____

Thank God—He always has healing for any deficient area in your marriage.

What good habits has God helped you cultivate to strengthen your marriage?

_____

_____

_____

Take—daily instruction from the Holy Spirit for your sake and for your marriage's sake.

What additional good habits might God want you to cultivate now?

_____

_____

_____

Straight from God

"So they are no longer two but one flesh. What therefore God has joined together, let not man separate." (Matthew 19:6)

Jesus made clear that no one should hinder or hurt a marriage, especially the husband and wife, themselves. Yet sometimes we have harmful habits we don't realize. Consider a time you made an adjustment in one area of your life that required adjustments in other areas. Since God is always at work in us, what one adjustment can you make that directly follows from God's current work in you?

_____

_____

_____

For Your Marriage (choose one or more)

Share today's Straight from God verse with your beloved. (Call, text, email, discuss.)

What actions have you and your mate taken that have strengthened your marriage? (Thank God.)

What actions have you and your mate taken that have weakened your marriage? (Confess, pray.)

With God's help, create a plan to eliminate one harmful habit in your marriage. (Commit in prayer, track progress.)

Ask God to reveal areas of your marriage that lack oneness and listen for His response. (Share, discuss.)

NOTES

_____

_____

_____

_____

_____

_____

_____

_____

_____

_____

_____

_____

_____

_____

_____

Week Three, Day Five

When You Want to Quit

I hate cooking. My version of heaven has perpetual room service, and the streets of gold are lined with tables of desserts, none of which I prepared. Here's why:

1. Cooking is messy. (Stuff goes *everywhere*. I drop things. I miss the bowl, or the pot, or whatever.)

2. Cooking takes so much time. (What? It's 5:30p.m., and I have to do it again? I did this twice today already.)

3. I'm seldom successful at cooking. (I usually fill the kitchen with smoke. So much so, my husband dismantled the nearest smoke detector. And, yes, I am that mother whose children thought it normal to cut the burnt bottoms off most cooked foods.)

4. I don't like feeling like a failure.

5. I don't like feeling like a failure.

6. I don't like feeling like a failure.

See the pattern?

None of us enjoy doing things we feel we fail at. We can make ourselves do them for a time, but at some point, we'll want to avoid them. Eventually, we'll *find* a way to avoid them, and we'll use it.

It's part of our human nature. Part of our fallen, human nature.

Chances are, you got married with the idea you'd be happier married than not. You fell in love, or thought you had, or thought marrying was God's will, or all of the above.

Why doesn't marriage go smoothly? Why don't we always behave as if we're in love? And why, *why* can't we figure out how to simply fix our problems and move forward to live happily ever after?

Marriage doesn't always go smoothly because both parties in a marriage are fallen and sinful, and other people's decisions affect our past, present, and future. And we can't simply fix our problems and move forward with perfection, because the problems don't stop coming. Tomorrow there will be new ones.

All these dynamics can leave us wishing we hadn't gotten married. No one enjoys feeling like a failure.

If you are struggling in your marriage, and especially if you've been struggling for a long time, you probably fight feeling like a failure. Even if you blame your mate for most of the problems, even if your partner is at fault for most of the problems, there are probably moments when you're alone or feel alone, that leave you considering your own behaviors.

Did I do enough? What did I do wrong? Why isn't this working? How do I *do* this?

When those questions become persistent and tormenting, you'll want to quit. I know I have.

In those moments, I encourage you to step back. Prayerfully consider the knotted ball of yarn that is your marriage and ask God to help you unravel it. The strands of conflict don't all come from the same place. They don't all happen for the same reasons.

Some problems you'll be able to circumvent. I've learned to plan the evening meal before lunchtime. That way, dinnertime doesn't sneak up on me.

Some problems will still crop up. I've learned to have a back-up meal, something I can prepare quickly when life gets in the way and dinner is already late.

Some problems you'll always need help with. I've learned to ask for help in the kitchen. I enlist help with the dishes, which means even when I make messes, cleaning up is easier.

Ask God which ones are totally on you. I make my own problems when I don't plan for dinner. That's on me. Which problems can you take care of with better planning and preparation?

Ask God which ones you can't do anything about. Sometimes the oven stops working or ingredients expire unexpectedly. A buffet of leftovers won't hurt anyone. It might not be preferred, but it'll do the job. Which problems do you need to live with for now while depending on God's perspective and power?

Finally, if you're working with God, extend to yourself the same grace He extends to you. He's already provided everything you need for your marriage to be healthy. Ask Him to show you the provision you need for each moment of each day.

In this world, we won't live happily ever after. But, with God's help, we can live happily *even* after—after the problem, the mistake, the defeat. God is all about happy endings.

Just for You

Think—reread this week's Scripture passage. God is the performer of miracles.

What miracle in Scripture most speaks to you? Why?

_____

_____

_____

Thank God—that He is never surprised by our need and loved us in our sinful state.

What miracle have you seen God perform in your life or the life of someone you know?

_____

_____

_____

Take—comfort knowing God is aware of our needs and is ready to meet them.

When are you most tempted to withhold love from others?

_____

_____

_____

Straight from God

They remembered that God was their rock, the Most High God their redeemer. (Psalm 78:35)

When there's distance or conflict in our marriage, the best thing we can do is remember who God is and who He is to us. God is our rock, our foundation. He is sturdy, unshaken, and stable. God is our Redeemer. He can heal, redeem, and restore anything when we submit to Him and His work in our lives. When has God been your rock and your redeemer? How can remembering these events help you pursue a healthy marriage when facing small and big challenges?

_____

_____

_____

For Your Marriage **(choose one or more)**

Share today's Straight from God verse with your mate. (Call, text, email, discuss.)

What miracle do you need from God today? (Share.)

What miracle does your beloved need from God today? (Ask.)

Pray as individuals and together about each other's needs. (Share.)

Ask God to expose an area of your life or marriage where you don't always remember to include Him and listen for His response. (Share, discuss.)

NOTES

_____

_____

_____

_____

_____

_____

_____

_____

_____

_____

_____

_____

_____

_____

_____

_____

_____

Quick Connection for the Weekend

Impact

Which topic from this week affected you the most? Why?

The Valentine's Day that wasn't   Are you divorced inside
If you were given horrible advice   When you want to quit
If you're in a tough season

_____

_____

_____

Deeper Connection

What part of Psalm 46 do you find most encouraging?

_____

_____

_____

How can this truth help you grow in God and in your marriage?

_____

_____

_____

What part of Psalm 46 do you find most convicting?

_____

_____

_____

What truth from this passage is hardest for you to grasp or practice? Why?

_____

_____

_____

The opening verses of Psalm 46 remind us who God is and encourage us not to fear even if catastrophe comes. What catastrophe do you most fear happening in your marriage? When does that fear most affect you?

_____

_____

_____

Verse 8 instructs us to observe God's work in our lives and in our world, and verse 9 states He "makes wars cease." Conflict in marriage can feel like a war. What do you feel has been or is the worst conflict in your marriage? Why?

_____

_____

_____

In verse 10 we are told "Be still, and know that I am God." Why do you think God would tell those facing trouble to worship Him? How does worship affect your attitude? Your perspective?

_____

_____

_____

Carry it Forward

What traits or works of God provoke you to worship? What provokes your mate to worship?

_____

_____

_____

What method of worship ministers most to you? To your spouse? (singing, verbal adoration, being quiet, observing nature, etc.)

_____

_____

_____

Pray Together:

This week set aside time to worship as individuals and as a couple in your home. Scripture promises when Jesus is lifted up, He will draw all men—all husbands and wives—to Himself. The closer you both get to God, the closer you will get to each other.

Begin and end your worship time with this prayer: Heavenly Father, we commit to trust You when trouble comes to our lives and marriage. Help us remember who You are, and therefore who we are, in times of peace and times of conflict. In Jesus's name. Amen.

PITFALLS

Scriptures for This Week (Matthew 4:1–11)

¹*Then Jesus was led up by the Spirit into the wilderness to be tempted by the devil.* ² *And after fasting forty days and forty nights, he was hungry.* ³ *And the tempter came and said to him, "If you are the Son of God, command these stones to become loaves of bread."* ⁴ *But he answered, "It is written, "'Man shall not live by bread alone, but by every word that comes from the mouth of God.'"* ⁵ *Then the devil took him to the holy city and set him on the pinnacle of the temple* ⁶ *and said to him, "If you are the Son of God, throw yourself down, for it is written, "'He will command his angels concerning you,' and "'On their hands they will bear you up, lest you strike your foot against a stone.'"* ⁷ *Jesus said to him, "Again it is written, 'You shall not put the Lord your God to the test.'"* ⁸ *Again, the devil took him to a very high mountain and showed him all the kingdoms of the world and their glory.* ⁹ *And he said to him, "All these I will give you, if you will fall down and worship me."* ¹⁰ *Then Jesus said to him, "Be gone, Satan! For it is written, "'You shall worship the Lord your God and him only shall you serve.'"* ¹¹ *Then the devil left him, and behold, angels came and were ministering to him.*

Why Many Marriages Fail within the First Five Years

By most conservative estimates, about 20 percent of all first marriages end in divorce within the first five years, and another 30 percent within the first ten.

I believe there are two reasons for this:

One, most folks who have children do so within the first five years. A marriage that might already be strained experiences a dramatic change. The husband and wife who were impatient with each other grow more impatient because of lack of sleep, financial burdens, less time to even try to concentrate on each other or address issues, the stress of becoming parents, hormonal and physiological changes in the wife, and a plethora of other relationship obstacles that come with the birth of a child.

The couple's relational reserve runs dry, and there's no opportunity to refill that reservoir. If this challenge is on top of others, the marriage becomes more tenuous. If this challenge is the first in the relationship, and neither has previous experience enduring hardship, the couple has no skills on which to draw. The birth of the child is the straw that breaks the camel's back, because the poor camel's back was already overloaded.

The marriage is left gasping for breath as the waters of strife rise, and they drown.

I believe the second primary reason so many marriages fail within the first five to ten years comes from a non-productive belief system most couples mistakenly cling to. Here's what I mean:

During the first year, you're in the honeymoon phase and (hopefully) little seems to be wrong.

By the second year, you begin to realize what isn't working.

By the third year, you decide what you're going to do about everything that isn't working.

By the fourth year, you realize few of your ideas work and finding solutions will take much longer than you expected.

And by the fifth year, you decide whether or not to stay.

This is where the road splits. There are those who call it quits in a way the world can see. They get a divorce. And there are those who divorce inwardly. They begin building walls and over time their hearts are so hidden behind a series of barriers the marriage dies a slow death inch by inch in their hearts. They wear the rings, but distance in the relationship grows.

Some folks stay in that "fifth year" phase. They are perpetually deciding whether or not to stay. And eventually, a portion of those choose to divorce.

When I've talked with couples, I've not found one person who actually enjoys a strife-filled marriage. Even complete jerks suffer their own hurts or bemusement when tensions abound and true connection is elusive. If we could choose, the vast majority of us would rather be in love, feel in love, live in love, and enjoy love with the person we love most, or at least the person we loved most at one time.

For me, the temptation to build walls, pull back, or let distance grow is often rooted in a cycle of disappointment and impatience. Then my enemy steps in with taunts. He says things like *It shouldn't be this way. By now, Stephen should know how to love you better.* Or some other remark that encourages me to be even more disappointed and make that disappointment the filter through which I view our life together.

For years I fell victim to this mentality. Yes, Stephen and I had some serious areas of disconnect. But the good stuff was hazed over by my wrong perspective.

Then I learned the snapshots of life the devil wanted me to concentrate on weren't compatible with God's vision for my marriage. God's vision is always long-term. He is patient and intentional and doesn't begrudge teaching us every day as His dear children. His plan for us as individuals is that we constantly grow more into the image of Christ. The same is true of our marriages.

On this side of heaven, we will never be done becoming more like Jesus. The same is true of our earthly union.

When a cycle of disappointment and impatience tempts us to divorce in deed or in our hearts, we can instead choose to embrace God's perspective. His long-term vision is always best. If we start there, we can overcome temptation just like Jesus did.

Just for You

Think—reread this week's Scripture passage. The enemy loves to target you and your marriage.

How does Satan attempt to discourage you in your life and marriage?

_____

_____

_____

Thank God—you can use His Word to combat the enemy's taunts, tricks, lies, and half-truths.

To what temptation of Jesus do you most relate? Why?

_____

_____

_____

Take—hold of Jesus's example and the truths of Scripture to use when you are tempted.

What Scriptures do you rely on when tempted to disbelieve God?

_____

_____

_____

Straight from God

"The thief comes only to steal and kill and destroy. I came that they may have life and have it abundantly." (John 10:10)

Since the enemy was bold enough to tempt the Son of God, no doubt he will come after us. He wants to steal all that is rightfully ours as believers, kill our dreams of having a healthy marriage, and destroy our families. He longs to discredit God's reputation by destroying the picture of Christ's relationship with the Church—marriage. What recent circumstance has the enemy used to create dissension in your marriage? How can you use Scripture to eliminate dissension and create unity?

_____

_____

_____

For Your Marriage (choose one or more)

Share today's Straight from God verse with your spouse. (Call, text, email, discuss.)

How is the enemy tempting you now, personally and in your marriage? (Share.)

How is the enemy tempting your mate now, personally and in your marriage? (Ask.)

What do you both need from God to recognize those temptations and overcome them? (Share, ask, discuss, pray.)

Ask God to reveal any area of your life and marriage that lack an abundance of the Holy Spirit and listen for His response. (Share, discuss.)

NOTES

_____
_____
_____
_____
_____
_____
_____
_____
_____
_____
_____
_____
_____
_____
_____

Week Four, Day Two

How Can I Get What I Want from My Marriage?

I once heard a minister, who'd been serving others for about forty years, advise a believer that the way to get what he wanted out of his marriage was to lay down ultimatums. The issues in the marriage weren't adultery, addiction, or the result of large character flaws. Rather, they basically involved lifestyle preferences and personality differences.

I'd known the couple for a long time, and I was aware of their history. I knew the husband was as much at fault as the wife for the miscommunications and tension in his marriage. They both had trauma they hadn't healed from. And neither had grown up seeing an example of biblical marriage. They wanted to be happy, but neither was willing to extend grace to the other while they learned together.

Often when I talk with people who are frustrated in their marriage, if frustration has built over time, either the husband or wife—or both—feel trapped. Our human tendency is to respond by setting boundaries we feel will protect us. We want to follow the previously mentioned awful advice and lay down ultimatums. "My way or the highway."

Even our culture teaches that self-discovery includes figuring out my own needs and wants, then demanding those needs and wants be met. Unfortunately, this idea will never get us the marriage we want. Positionally, making demands puts me at odds with my mate. Yes, we are face-to-face, but we're looking in opposite directions.

Amos 3:3 poses the question "Do two walk together, unless they have agreed to meet?"

Making demands won't get me what I want from my marriage. Getting what I want from my marriage requires changing what I want so it's in line with God's plan and in agreement with my spouse. Then, we pursue *that*, together.

I've learned the hard way that, when my husband and I have different goals, we're at risk of working at odds with each other. We're like two people pulling on opposite ends of a rope. We get nowhere. We get tired and ornery. And sooner or later, resentment and dissension arise.

But if we work together, if we have the same goal, the same vision for our marriage—a vision that comes from God—we both get what we want, and God blesses our efforts.

Are you at odds with your mate? Are you tired of fighting? Tired of being dissatisfied?

If the tension is over something petty, ask God why that's such a big deal to you. If it's tied to a wound, seek healing. If it's tied to a preconceived idea, be willing to reassess. If it's tied to pride, or guilt, or shame, or some other harmful thought pattern, work with God to replace that trait with the Fruit of the Spirit.

Establishing unity in your marriage will bring the satisfaction you long for, and it's up to you to take the first step.

Just for You

Think—reread this week's Scripture passage. Being in unity means having the same ideas, desires, plans, and goals. In essence, looking in the same direction.

What goals has God given you as an individual?

_____

_____

_____

Thank God—He knows your life from beginning to end.

What do you need from God to pursue His goals for you?

_____

_____

_____

Take—guidance from Scripture, the Holy Spirit in you, prayer, and wise counsel.

Which of these do you usually turn to when making decisions and setting goals? Why?

_____

_____

_____

Straight from God

Set your minds on things that are above, not on things that are on earth. ³For you have died, and your life is hidden with Christ in God. ⁴When Christ who is your life appears, then you also will appear with him in glory. (Colossians 3:2–4)

When we're tired, worried, burdened, stressed, hurt, or discontent, it's easy to focus on how our lives are less than perfect and take our eyes off God and eternity. This is why Scripture encourages us to view our lives in light of Christ and our future in heaven. What aspect of heaven do you most look forward to?

_____

_____

_____

For Your Marriage (choose one or more)

Share today's Straight from God verse with your mate. (Call, text, email, discuss.)

What areas of your marriage do you feel have the most unity? What areas have the least unity? (Share, discuss.)

What areas of your marriage does your mate feel have the most unity? What areas have the least unity? (Ask.)

How can having an eternal perspective facilitate unity in your marriage? (Share, ask, discuss, pray.)

Ask God to help you recognize when your mind is on earthly things rather on things that are above and listen for His response. (Share, discuss.)

NOTES

_____
_____
_____
_____
_____
_____
_____
_____
_____
_____
_____
_____
_____
_____
_____

Week Four, Day Three

Are You Angry Your Mate Isn't Telepathic?

I must confess, this is a pet peeve of mine. Sorry, ladies, but we women are the *worst* at having and perpetuating this mentality, as we share and sympathize with each other about the trouble in our marriages. (I know I'm guilty.)

The *by now he should know what I need* mentality.

For whatever reason—maybe from Disney movies, or fairy tales, or romance novels, I don't know—we get the idea that being married flips a mental switch and enables our husbands to read our minds. We think that because our mates say they love us, they should *know* what we want and need.

When this thought continues to its ultimate conclusion, our thinking veers to a dangerous place. If my mate doesn't know what I need, he doesn't love me.

Then, too often we close up, close off, and stand aside with our arms crossed waiting on our mates to become telepathic, and growing angry at them when they aren't. Some of us spew accusations. Some of us give the silent treatment. Others of us shrink into a corner and pity ourselves. I'm guilty of all of these.

God, in His kindness, spoke to me about these bad habits. In my spirit I heard *Shellie, you're killing your marriage*. Then He led me to two biblical passages. The first is Matthew 6:8, the verse right before Jesus teaches us how to pray. He says "your Father knows what you need before you ask him." And I realized, if we as believers are commanded to pray and ask for what we need *even though God already knows*, then the act of prayer is about more than we understand. Something else is happening, even in the spirit realm. And, if we're commanded to ask God who already know our needs, how much more should we be willing to ask a human being as flawed as we are?

The second passage God led me to is 1 Peter 3:7. "Likewise, husbands, live with your wives in an understanding way, showing honor to the woman as the weaker vessel, since they are heirs with you of the grace of life, so that your prayers may not be hindered."

The King James Version says husbands are to "dwell with them" (their wives) "according to knowledge."

If we consider the time and culture 1 Peter was written in, we see God is changing the status quo. He's explaining women should no longer be considered voiceless possessions or less than men. Rather, women are heirs of all God has to offer right alongside men. However, it also means since women have a voice, they should use it to strengthen the marriage.

When God showed me these passages together, I understood why He'd told me I was killing my marriage. By expecting Stephen to read my mind, by withholding from him my wants and needs, I was *keeping* from him the very information he needed to obey God. I was responsible for teaching Stephen about me—which meant I needed to know the truth of who I was, my wounds, my sin, my ignorance, and the challenges I face every day. The burden of being spiritually self-aware and transparent is on me.

God was calling me to let myself be known. Stephen couldn't read my mind, and God didn't ask him to.

Rather, as a godly wife I'm called to pay attention to my wants and needs and share them with my husband. I'm called to share my deepest dreams and private yearnings. I share my past, present, and future with him. I teach him about me—with love, patience, and grace, not resenting that he doesn't "get" me all at once—admitting that I am still learning *myself*, too.

Of course, this sharing of knowledge goes both ways. As believers, we owe it to ourselves to look at any dissatisfaction we have in our marriages and ask ourselves (and God) if *we* are the reason.

My husband isn't a mind reader. God didn't create him to be, nor does God ask him to be.

I have no right to hold him to a standard not even God expects. And if I do, I harm my marriage.

Just for You

Think—reread this week's Scripture passage. Consider that God knows our needs yet commands us to pray and present our needs to Him.

What wants and needs are most pressing to you now? Why?

_____

_____

_____

Thank God—for always hearing your prayers.

What wants and needs do you find most difficult to discuss with God?

_____

_____

_____

Take—direction from God about when and how to voice your wants and needs to your beloved.

What wants and needs do you find most difficult to discuss with your mate?

_____

_____

_____

Straight from God

Pray without ceasing, (1 Thessalonians 5:17)

Scripture tells us to be in constant conversation with God. We are to go to God first with our wants and needs. This eliminates the possibility of expecting our mates to meet a need God is supposed to meet. How can following this command in Scripture remove stress from your marriage?

_____

_____

_____

For Your Marriage (choose one or more)

Share today's Straight from God verse with your beloved. (Call, text, email, discuss.)

What want or need do you need your beloved to meet now? (Share.)

What want or need does your spouse need you to meet now? (Ask.)

Discuss how you've met each other's needs in the past. (Thank each other.)

Ask God to help you recognize when you stop praying or communicating with Him, then listen for His response. (Share, discuss.)

NOTES

_____

_____

_____

_____

_____

_____

_____

_____

_____

_____

_____

_____

_____

_____

_____

_____

_____

_____

Week Four, Day Four

Have You Put a Time Limit on God?

We'd been friends for a few years. We had children the same age, and we both loved our husbands.

But her husband was going through something. He worked, came home, and basically ignored her. He never initiated conversation. They lived as roommates.

She did everything for their family and home. She worked part-time, cared for their children, balanced the checkbook, and even mowed the yard. She felt she had no choice. If she didn't do those things, they wouldn't get done.

Her husband wasn't lazy, he just didn't … engage with her. He wasn't purposely cruel or abusive. Rather, even when he was present, he was absent.

She couldn't take it any longer. She wanted more for their son—a close relationship with his father. More for their daughter—the same. She wanted more for herself, and she'd grown impatient living with this man, waiting for him to actually do the things they'd talked about and agreed on before and during their marriage.

They had agreement, but nothing was happening. Like, the blueprint was there, but construction hadn't begun.

She called me, wanting advice. The pressure inside her had built so much, she was ready to leave him. In fact, she'd packed, made other living arrangements, and was going to leave him *that day.*

They both professed to be believers. Knowing I might lose my friend if I told her the truth (yes, it's happened to me many times), I told her the truth. I knew nothing else would help her.

Me: He's not cheating on you?
My friend: No.
Me: He still wants to be married?
My friend: Yes.

Me: He's not abusive, using drugs, harming you or the children?

My friend: No.

Me: What's the main reason you want to leave?

My friend: Because I feel like my life, my children's lives, are passing by. I'm tired of waiting on the life we agreed to build together.

Me: If an angel appeared before you right now, and told you it would take another ten years, five months, two weeks, and four days for this change to happen, would you stay? Don't answer that. Think about it. If you knew there would eventually be the payoff you want for staying, would you stay?

My friend: (After a long silence.) Yes.

Me: Then, you're putting a time limit on God. Your husband's got his own issues. What if you set aside your disappointment, seek to love him more in spite of his failings, and ask God what you need to do to help God's work in your husband and your marriage?

The problem in my friend's marriage wasn't her goals. She had great goals. Godly goals.

But somewhere along the line, she'd put a time limit on those goals. When they didn't happen, she hoarded the hurts. Those hurts became the reasons she no longer wanted to be married.

Part of the joy of preparing for marriage and experiencing the early days of marriage is dreaming of and planning your life together. Those goals and that vision have a lovely shine. We aim for that, which can be good. Unfortunately, we often tend to put a timeline on that vision, and that can be harmful.

My timeline isn't always God's timeline. As believers, we openly say that about external issues, but what about our marriage?

God was working behind the scenes, and I didn't even know it. How many times do we look back at experiences in life and find comfort from this perspective about job opportunities, people we meet, even difficult seasons? Again, what about in our marriage?

I need to walk by faith, not by sight.

You know what I'm going to say. We'll encourage ourselves with these words as we face spiritual challenges, but what about regarding our marriage?

Have you put a time limit on God? I know I've done it countless times.

Even regarding a godly goal. Even regarding a goal God led you to set. Is that time limit threatening your marriage, because as time has passed you've begun to view your spouse through a filter of disappointment?

Maybe you need to lay down your goals. If they're messing up your vision, let them go. They're hindering you.

Rather, ask God to help you view your spouse as He does. Consider your spouse's deepest need as God does. Seek to meet that need as God does.

I know you might be tired and weary. I get it. I've been there.

Still, I ask you, if an angel appeared to you today and told you how long it would take for your goals to be reached, would you stay? Would you stay open and love your mate in the meantime?

By the way, my friend stayed. And it took almost ten more years, but they've built the marriage they always wanted.

Just for You

Think—reread this week's Scripture passage. Since my relationship with God is my example for my marriage, every skill I learn in my relationship with God can be used in my marriage.

When have you had to wait on God to fulfill a promise?

_____

_____

_____

Thank God—that even when waiting hurts, His timing is perfect.

What are you waiting on God to do in and for you?

_____

_____

_____

Take—strength from the knowledge that God has a long-term vision for us. He will perform His work in His children, no matter how long that work takes.

What long-term work has God done in you? What long-term work is God doing in you now?

_____

_____

_____

Straight from God

But you, O Lord, are a God merciful and gracious, slow to anger and abounding in steadfast love and faithfulness. (Psalm 86:15)

The King James Version of this verse uses the phrase "long suffering" to describe God's attitude toward us. He understands we are still learning about Him and how to be in relationship with Him. What aspect of God's character do you most depend on as you learn more about Him?

_____

_____

_____

For Your Marriage (choose one or more)

Share today's Straight from God verse with your spouse. (Call, text, email, discuss.)

What promises are you waiting on God to fulfill? What promises are you waiting on your mate to fulfill? (Share, discuss.)

What promises is your mate waiting on God to fulfill? What promises is your mate waiting on you to fulfill? (Ask.)

How do God's grace and faithfulness manifest His love? (Share, ask, discuss.)

Ask God to reveal where you lack faithfulness to Him and your mate, then listen for His response. (Share, discuss.)

NOTES

_____

_____

_____

_____

_____

_____

_____

_____

_____

_____

_____

_____

_____

_____

_____

_____

Week Four, Day Five

Is Pride Killing Your Marriage?

Their marriage looked perfect. A young couple, both in their second marriage.

Both had been deeply hurt in their first marriages. The first marriages had ended after a short time, because of blatant sin on the other party's part. They'd both been betrayed at the deepest level. So, they each understood that pain. They didn't enter this second marriage without careful consideration. Neither of them wanted to be hurt that way again.

The second marriage should have been a dream. They were both believers. They had godly parents supporting them. The wife even worked as her pastor's secretary.

By accident, I learned their marriage was in trouble. She hadn't meant for me to know. But during a conversation, a piece of a comment caught my attention, and suddenly I understood why she tended to avoid eye contact with me. The other things she'd said (and hadn't said) to me over many months took on a different meaning, and I recognized them as a smoke screen.

Their marriage was a mess. A colossal mess, and she was hiding it from everyone.

I questioned her, encouraged her to talk to their families for support and help, and to tell her pastor, so he could help them get counseling and pray for them.

She refused. "I can't tell my boss."

She couldn't tell her boss—her pastor—that her marriage was in trouble.

Why? She was embarrassed. She didn't want people, especially her pastor, to know.

The marriage struggled for years. Years!

Finally, late one year, they separated (of course). She called me because she wanted my support in getting a divorce. No infidelity, no abuse, no addictions, or other serious problems were present. They had issues, but don't we all?

I had to tell her the truth. And, yes, this was one of the many times in my life I've had to tell someone the truth, knowing it could, and probably would, end the friendship.

I told her if she didn't have scriptural grounds for divorce, she was walking in blatant disobedience to God. I told her, their children would pay the price for her decision for the rest of their lives.

Her response? "Oh, we've already talked about Christmas."

What??? Then, she told me their plan.

Her husband would move back in for Christmas, and they would pretend all was fine. They didn't want to ruin their children's Christmas with an impending divorce.

I asked her, "If the two of you can work together to lie to the children through December, why can't you work together to fix your marriage?"

She hung up. I lost a friend.

She was living a lie, pretending all was fine when at church. But she was hurting herself. They were hurting each other with the Christmas charade. They were hurting their testimony. Most of all, they were hurting their children. Their children saw the hypocrisy. Their children felt the tension. In effect, they were teaching their children to lie, all because of pride. Their pride was more important than their children's future.

My (then) friend refused to face the fear and hurts that were the roots of her pride. In her case, the pride covered a fear that if she really looked at her life, if she really examined all the negative feelings she had about her life (not only her marriage), others would think less of her. Abandon her.

Where did those roots of abandonment come from? Her own parents' divorce.

I am vulnerable. All of us are vulnerable—to repeat the behavior that wounded us.

Why? Because until that wound is healed, it is always in our vision. We can't help but steer our lives toward it. Even if we don't repeat the exact behavior, until we process that wound and choose a different focus all our judgments and actions will be based on what we haven't yet surrendered to God.

I beg you. Don't let pride, or what looks like pride, destroy your marriage.

If you're having trouble, get help.

If you're not having trouble, learn in advance, grow your love, because—trust me—struggles will come. You owe it to yourself, to your mate, to your children, to fix the problems inside yourself, rather than carrying them through life into every relationship you have, including the one with your children.

If we ask Him, listen, and obey, God will walk us through every step.

Just for You

Think—reread this week's Scripture passage. Often fear and pride go hand in hand.

In what areas of your life do you battle fear and pride?

_____

_____

_____

Thank God—you don't have to hide the truth of your life from Him.

What aspects of your life have you hesitated to discuss with God? Why?

_____

_____

_____

Take—instruction from God's Word that pride will only harm your life, your marriage, and your family.

How can you address the cycle of pride and fear in your life? What do you need from God to do that?

_____

_____

_____

Straight from God

Pride goes before destruction, and a haughty spirit before a fall. (Proverbs 16:18)

Pride isolates us. It keeps us from being honest with God and others. It keeps us from asking for help and counsel. Believers weren't meant to journey through life alone. We are to confess our faults to each other and pray for each other. What burden and prayer need do you need to share with a believer you trust?

_____

_____

_____

For Your Marriage (choose one or more)

Share today's Straight from God verse with your spouse. (Call, text, email, discuss.)
What fears keep you from seeking help when you need it? (Share.)
What fears keep your spouse from seeking help? (Ask.)
In what area of your life might God be exposing pride? How can you find godly counsel regarding that area? (Share, discuss, pray.)
In what area of your mate's life might God be exposing pride? How can they find godly counsel regarding that area? (Ask, discuss, pray.)
Ask God to reveal habits that are based in pride or fear, then listen for His response. (Share, discuss.)

NOTES

_____
_____
_____
_____
_____
_____
_____
_____
_____
_____
_____
_____
_____
_____

Quick Connection for the Weekend

Impact

Which topic from this week affected you the most? Why?

Why most marriages fail   Have you put a time limit on God
How can I get what I want   Is pride killing your marriage
Anger at your non-telepathic mate

_____

_____

_____

Deeper Connection

What part of Matthew 4:1–11 do you find most encouraging?

_____

_____

_____

How can this truth help you grow in God and in your marriage?

_____

_____

_____

What part of Matthew 4:1–11 do you find most convicting?

_____

_____

_____

What do you need from God to righteously respond to that conviction?

_____

_____

_____

Satan's first temptation of Jesus referenced his weakness—his hunger and need for food. The enemy knows how to target our weaknesses and most pressing needs, to challenge our faith. What immediate need do you have right now, and how are you depending on God to meet it?

_____

_____

_____

In the second temptation, Satan twists Scripture to suit his own purpose. When we read the Bible, we must depend on the Holy Spirit to speak to our spirits and reveal the truth of Scripture to us. What Scriptures have you seen used incorrectly or out of context? How did that experience affect you?

_____

_____

_____

In the third temptation, the enemy promised to give Jesus what was, in truth, already His. One aspect of this temptation regards dependence. Another aspect is impatience. Satan tempted Christ to depend on him rather than on His relationship with the Father, and to take a misleading shortcut to get to His destination. Describe a time you knew you were tempted to depend on yourself or a method, rather than following God's process for your life.

_____

_____

_____

Carry it Forward

What is one thing you need from your mate to help you respond to God's conviction in your life?

_____

_____

_____

What is one thing you can do for your mate to help them respond to God's conviction in their life?

_____

_____

_____

Pray together:

Heavenly Father, Thank You for your Word that helps us fight temptation and the enemy's lies. Help us learn your truth, remember your truth, and use your truth when we are tempted, both as individuals and in our marriage. In Jesus's name. Amen.

TRUTHS

Scriptures for This Week (Psalm 34)

[1] I will bless the Lord at all times; his praise shall continually be in my mouth. [2] My soul makes its boast in the Lord; let the humble hear and be glad. [3] Oh, magnify the Lord with me, and let us exalt his name together! [4] I sought the Lord, and he answered me and delivered me from all my fears. [5] Those who look to him are radiant, and their faces shall never be ashamed. [6] This poor man cried, and the Lord heard him and saved him out of all his troubles. [7] The angel of the Lord encamps around those who fear him, and delivers them. [8] Oh, taste and see that the Lord is good! Blessed is the man who takes refuge in him! [9] Oh, fear the Lord, you his saints, for those who fear him have no lack! [10] The young lions suffer want and hunger; but those who see the Lord lack no good thing. [11] Come, O children, listen to me; I will teach you the fear of the Lord. [12] What man is there who desires life and loves many days, that he may see good? [13] Keep your tongue from evil and your lips from speaking deceit. [14] Turn away from evil and do good; seek peace and pursue it. [15] The eyes of the Lord are toward the righteous and his ears toward their cry. [16] The face of the Lord is against those who do evil, to cut off the memory of them from the earth. [17] When the righteous cry for help, the Lord hears and delivers them out of all their troubles. [18] The Lord is near to the brokenhearted and saves the crushed in spirit. [19] Many are the afflictions of the righteous, but the Lord delivers him out of them all. [20] He keeps all his bones; not one of them is broken. [21] Affliction will slay the wicked, and those who hate the righteous will be condemned. [22] The Lord redeems *the life of his servants; none of those who take refuge in him will be condemned.*

Week Five, Day One

What Your Marriage Vows Really Mean— No Matter What Words You Use

My oldest son married a fantastic, godly woman. Can you tell I love her?

The wedding was beautiful (of course), my new daughter-in-law was stunningly beautiful (she still is, inside and out), and my oldest was … captivated. From the moment his bride entered the room, no one existed for him except her and the minister officiating the ceremony.

This mama's heart nearly burst with fulfillment, with joy, with gratitude to God for guiding my son's steps to meet the woman who was right then becoming his wife.

I sat there soaking in every second and blotting away happy tears, hoping I'd taught him enough. Hoping I'd given him the right foundation to start this season of his life fully equipped, fully prepared, and fully aware to meet the commitment he was making.

I thought, *Dear son, did I adequately teach you what your marriage vows really mean?* Had I made sure he understood no matter the words used, the bottom line is the same?

Yes, marriage vows include promises. They contain words like "to love and to cherish," "for richer or poorer," and "in sickness and in health, until death do us part." Our son and his bride added their own personal vows, specifics they promised each other before God and witnesses. Yet at the center, at the core of those vows, is a truth all engaged and married couples need to understand and embrace.

What our marriage vows really mean is:

We're committing to trust our mate's relationship with God.

And we're vowing to consciously and consistently grow our own relationship with God.

Keeping the commitment, fulfilling the vows, *demands* this.

I can't love and cherish without God's help. I can't handle the pressure, the stress of living richer or poorer, without God's strength. I can't give or receive the love my mate needs "in sickness and in health," without a constant infusion of God's power.

I can't do marriage well—give and love, cling and support, honor and serve, become one with my mate—until the day God calls one of us to Himself, without supernatural intervention. Life's too hard. During our thirty-seven plus years of marriage, my husband and I have faced:

Job loss multiple times. Church loss. Loss of friends. Loss of our home.

Having a child with a birth defect and medical challenges. A child who currently lives as a spiritual prodigal.

In the early 2000s, almost three years of me having debilitating symptoms including intermittent paralysis on one side.

A work schedule for my husband that required me to homeschool our children, rather than working full time outside the home (a significant blow to our finances), if we wanted our children to have any time with their father.

Betrayal by fellow believers who claimed to love and support us.

Both of us trying to overcome emotional wounds from our childhood.

Both of us working through the trauma of sexual abuse.

Both of us filtering through what we learned in church while growing up, working to figure out what we learned wrong and what we learned right.

We've moved sixteen times so far, and, no, my husband isn't in the military.

A recent diagnosis for me of autoimmune disease that often affects my ability to walk.

If I couldn't have asked God how to handle every step, I don't know what I would have done. I know we wouldn't have made it this far. Our marriage wouldn't have survived, let alone thrived. I would have messed it up, screwed it up, *burned* it up, or even walked away.

Because deep inside I'm carnal. I'm selfish. I want things I can't or shouldn't have.

I'm not taking full credit for the condition of my marriage, obviously my husband had to make decisions and take actions of his own. But I do take full responsibility for my portion of my marriage.

Do you? Do you take full responsibility for your portion of your marriage?

What are you doing to meet that responsibility? In the day-in and day-out stuff and when crisis strikes. When was the last time you asked God what He wants from your marriage during the next week or the coming year? The last time you asked God what He wants your marriage to look like to your children, your family, and those you influence? As believers, presenting ourselves to God as a "living sacrifice" includes our married life.

Whether you're in the first few years of marriage as my son and his bride are, or if you've been married for decades, it's never too late to put God at the center of your marriage.

In truth, for God to be at the center of your marriage, He must be the center of your life.

Just for You

Think—reread this week's Scripture passage. Your marriage vows mean you commit to grow your relationship with God and trust your beloved to do the same.

What phrase from your marriage vows is most important to you right now?

_____

_____

_____

Thank God—for His constant efforts to work in you and your mate.

What evidence of His work do you see in yourself? In your mate?

_____

_____

_____

Take—heart that God has already provided everything you need to grow your relationship with Him.

What do you need today to grow your relationship with God?

_____

_____

_____

Straight from God

His divine power has granted to us all things that pertain to life and godliness, through the knowledge of him who called us to his own glory and excellence, (2 Peter 1:3)

God's glory and goodness call us to Him, but we receive all we need to live a godly life "through the knowledge of him." What do you know about God that helps you grow in Him?

_____

_____

_____

For Your Marriage (choose one or more)

Share today's Straight from God verse with your spouse. (Call, text, email, discuss.)

In what area do you need to put more effort into your relationship with God? (Share.)

In what area does your mate need to put more effort into their relationship with God? (Ask.)

What is the condition of your relationship with God, and why is it in that state? (Share, discuss.)

What is the condition of your mate's relationship with God, and why is it in that state? (Ask, discuss.)

What provision does Christ's sacrifice offer believers, and how can that provision benefit your marriage? (Share, ask, discuss.)

Ask God to help you receive and utilize all the benefits of following Him and listen for His response. (Share, discuss.)

NOTES

_____
_____
_____
_____
_____
_____
_____
_____
_____
_____
_____

Week Five, Day Two

Men and Women Are Not Opposites

Go ahead and laugh. When I was a little girl—like, really little—I thought dogs were boys and cats were girls. And that's how we got dogs and cats.

I don't know exactly why I thought that. I'd never seen a litter with both dogs (boys) and cats (girls). I was quite taken aback when I realized I was mistaken.

Perhaps my misperception came from that expression about folks "fighting like cats and dogs." Get it? A couple who doesn't get along fights like cats and dogs? I guess I figured the dog and cat in question were married—one's a boy and one's a girl. It simply didn't occur to me how very different dogs and cats are.

If you remember the main idea from week one, you know I'm of the opinion there's only one, true blanket rule in marriage: Live righteously.

But, how can I do that when my spouse is so unlike me? you ask. *When I don't understand them? When it seems as if we are more different than cats and dogs?*

I understand why you think that. I get it, I do. Especially if those differences (not sins, differences) cause tension, arguments, misunderstandings, and communication problems.

What I offer is a change in perspective.

Men and women are not opposites. We are two pieces of the same puzzle. The proof of this truth is found in Genesis 1:27: "So God created man in his own image, in the image of God he created him; male and female he created them."

You've probably seen this verse many times. Take a new look, and you'll notice the repetition. God really wants us to grasp the concept that both men and women are made in God's image. This means we're not opposites. Rather, I have some traits of God my husband doesn't have, and he has traits of God I don't have.

Men and women are not opposites trying to find common ground. We are individual creatures that lack a part of God's character before marriage, then spend our married lives learning to appreciate, embrace, and utilize the parts of God's character we don't have, that manifest in our mate.

I've heard teaching on marriage that starts with celebrating our differences. Sounds like a good idea.

I've heard teaching on marriage suggesting we adapt to the differences in our mate. Maybe that could work.

But what if we simply change our perspective? Instead of looking at our differences as an obstacle—or worse, a foreign body we have to assimilate—what if we look for ways our mate is just like God?

Sound strange? Guess what: The parts of your spouse's character and thought patterns you don't understand might closely correlate with the parts of God's character you don't understand and have difficulty embracing. Consider the spouse who operates from a place of mercy, versus the spouse who gravitates toward judgment. The spouse who is creative or spontaneous, versus the spouse who makes intricate, long-term plans. What appear to be personality traits or even differences in how we think as individuals, might be mild—or extreme—manifestations of God's character.

Try this: The traits (not sins) in your beloved that are different from yours—research them in Scripture. Look for instances in which God the Father, Jesus, or the Holy Spirit manifest those same traits. Then ask God to teach you about those parts of Himself, so you can learn to appreciate them in Him and in your beloved.

If fear arises, pray about that fear to figure out why you're afraid. If you're still uncomfortable, pray about that discomfort and find out what's blocking you from embracing that particular quality.

You were both created in God's image. You're two pieces of the same puzzle. With God's help, with insight and healing, you can learn to fit together, creating a beautiful and complete picture of God Himself.

Just for You

Think—reread this week's Scripture passage. God designed both you and your mate in His image.

What parts of you and your personality most reflect God?

_____

_____

_____

Thank God—for the parts of His character He placed within you.

What parts of your mate are different than you, yet reflect God's character?

_____

_____

_____

Take—relief from the truth your mate doesn't have to be like you, for the two of you to become one.

What conflicts in your marriage could be resolved if you saw God in the parts of your spouse that aren't like you?

_____

_____

_____

Straight from God

Thus says the Lord, your Redeemer, who formed you from the womb: "I am the Lord, who made all things, who alone stretched out the heavens, who spread out the earth by myself," (Isaiah 44:24)

Imagine God creating you. Imagine God creating your beloved. What do you think God had in mind when He planned for the two of you to become one?

_____

_____

_____

For Your Marriage (choose one or more)

Share today's Straight from God verse with your mate. (Call, text, email, discuss.)

What part of your character do you struggle with the most? Is this trait like God?

(Share, discuss.)

What part of your mate's character causes them the most struggle? Is this trait like God? (Ask, discuss.)

When has your marriage benefited from a difference between you and your beloved? (Share, discuss.)

Ask God to show you more of His character and attributes He placed in you and listen for His response. (Share, discuss.)

NOTES

_____

_____

_____

_____

_____

_____

_____

_____

_____

_____

_____

_____

_____

_____

How Can I Cultivate Kindness, Tenderness, and Forgiveness in My Marriage?

If it hasn't happened yet, there will come a time when irritation, dislike, or even hatred rears its ugly head in your marriage. There will be moments when love seems far away, forgotten, dead, and impossible to regain. When that happens, you have a choice.

As believers, we know we're supposed to forgive. We're supposed to be kind. We're not supposed to return evil for evil. We're supposed to love.

As married believers, we have an even greater call for our marriages to be a picture of Christ's relationship with and love for the Church.

How can we do this? How can we cultivate kindness, tenderness, and forgiveness when tensions rise? When you'd rather not see your mate's face? When you've wounded each other?

Asking for forgiveness isn't enough. We have to be able to extend true forgiveness, as Ephesians 4:32 commands: "Be kind to one another, tenderhearted, forgiving one another, as God in Christ forgave you."

That's a tall order, isn't it, when we're hurt and angry? If hatred has entered the relationship, it's even tougher.

Fortunately, Ephesians 4:31 tells us how to prepare our hearts, so we can extend the true forgiveness Ephesians 4:32 commands. "Let all bitterness and wrath and anger and clamor and slander be put away from you, along with all malice."

I have work to do in my heart before I can truly forgive. I have to deal with any and all of the following:

Bitterness. Resentment. The sneer in my heart at my mate. The bad taste in my mouth at seeing, touching, speaking to, or acknowledging the existence of my mate.

Maybe you've never fought resentment, but I sure have.

Wrath. Explosive anger. Rage. The hair-trigger response where we go from slight disdain to complete loathing in less than half a second.

I've been there.

Anger. A simmering mad that smolders long after the incident.

Yep, this one, too.

Clamor. Actual screaming or a loud quarrel. Brawling with words. The noise in your head. Your willful repetition of your mate's faults (spoken or unspoken), to the point the litany becomes background music in your everyday life.

I am guilty. Totally guilty.

Slander. Abusive words. Blanket statements and negative generalizations. Words intended to harm, demean, or embarrass.

Jesus, help me. I'm guilty of this one, too.

Malice. Spitefulness. Behavior other than speech intended to harm or injure. Joy at your spouse's suffering. Pure meanness.

Without Jesus working in me and changing me, I have no hope. But with Jesus, I can learn to rid myself of all of these, so I can truly be kind to my husband, tender-hearted to him, and forgive.

Sometimes the decision is quick and easy.

Sometimes it means digging in with God and getting healing for long-term, deep hurts. The wound I received from my mate hit a button in me that I've not yet conquered. God and I have work to do.

If—like I was—you were taught how to hold onto anger. How to manipulate others. If you didn't feel safe growing up. If you were abandoned in some way, rejected, betrayed, or learned from how others treated you that you were disposable or unimportant, this type of heart cleaning might be more difficult for you—it certainly has been for me. Because today's wound from my spouse makes me feel the same way I did when I was previously wounded by someone else.

Either way, whether it's a quick healing process or a lengthy one, healing is completely possible with God's help and leading. But we have to prepare our hearts.

I encourage you to start with the Lord's Prayer found in Matthew 6:9-13. That's where God started with me. Praying this prayer helped me begin learning the right perspective. Pray it as many times as needed and ask God to write it on your heart.

Extending true forgiveness is key in having a healthy marriage. Today, prayerfully consider whether you need to forgive, even if the hurt occurred many years ago. Then, work with God to cultivate kindness, tenderness, and forgiveness in your life, so you and your mate can enjoy the benefits.

Just for You

Think—reread this week's Scripture passage. Consider all God has forgiven you.

What does His forgiveness teach you about His love for you?

_____
_____
_____

Thank God—for His forgiveness, that Christ's work on the Cross is a complete work providing forgiveness for all your sin.

If you were in God's place, which of your sins would you find hardest to forgive? Why?

_____
_____
_____

Take—God's freely-offered forgiveness.

What sins or weaknesses do you need to confess to God now?

_____
_____
_____

Straight from God

But God shows his love for us in that while we were still sinners, Christ died for us. (Romans 5:8)

Spend time considering that God did everything necessary to have a close relationship with you before you knew Him. Have you ever given to someone in this manner out of love, knowing they could never repay you? What did that action do in your heart?

_____
_____
_____

For Your Marriage (choose one or more)

Share today's Straight from God verse with your beloved. (Call, text, email, discuss.)

Confess to your mate any sin God is convicting in you. (Share, discuss.)

What sin is God convicting in your mate? (Ask.)

If you and your spouse aren't already spiritual accountability partners, why? (Share, discuss, prayerfully consider.)

Ask God to teach you how to give *first* in an area of your marriage you might not want to give first and listen for His response. (Share, discuss.)

NOTES

_____

_____

_____

_____

_____

_____

_____

_____

_____

_____

_____

_____

_____

_____

_____

_____

_____

Week Five, Day Four

Why Is Marriage So Hard?

Haven't we all asked this question? How long were you married before you had your first disagreement? A month? A week? An hour?

Ours took place on our honeymoon, although no harsh words were exchanged. I disagreed with my husband about something, but I didn't say anything.

First, I told myself it didn't matter. It did.

Then, I told myself it wouldn't matter later. It did.

Then, I told myself I'd set it aside and it wouldn't matter, eventually. I set it aside, but it festered and grew and became a problem I couldn't be quiet about. And that issue, that singular event was a glimpse at what would be a huge problem in my marriage.

Chances are you've faced a big problem or two in your marriage. Why is that? Why, even if we're both Christians, even if we really, truly love each other, do we have all this conflict? Why is marriage so hard?

Marriage is hard because we live in a fallen world. A pat answer, I know, but that pretty well covers it. What that means is, I am fallen. I'm carnal, sinful, selfish, etc., and without God's help that's all I'll be. That equals my sin.

And, because I live in this fallen world with others who are fallen, their sinful behavior often hurts me. That equals my wounds.

So, when two people get married, the sins of both and the wounds of both come together to live in the same place at the same time. Doesn't sound promising, does it?

Except God is there, too. He uses circumstances, disagreements, and problems to reveal our weaknesses and our sin, so He can help us with them. He uses circumstances, disagreements, and problems to reveal our wounds, so He can heal them.

Marriage is hard because it's God's primary mechanism for provoking growth in married believers. It's what God uses to teach us, change us, and push us to be more like Him. My weaknesses hit my husband's, head-on. My wounds hit my husband's, head-on. My sin pushes my husband's buttons and vice versa.

Being married pushes us. Our love pushes us. God Himself pushes us to change and become more like Christ, in how we treat each other, how we think, and how we live together. And that's a good thing. Being conformed to the image of Christ is a good thing.

Is marriage hard? It sure can be.

Can it be the best thing to happen for our spiritual growth? Absolutely.

Just for You

Think—reread this week's Scripture passage. God's priority is your relationship with Him and making you more like Jesus.

What do you most admire about Jesus's life here on earth?

_____

_____

_____

Thank God—for Jesus's example in Scripture.

What do you think were Jesus's toughest moments here on earth? Why?

_____

_____

_____

Take—assurance from the knowledge God won't stop working in you, and He has a long-term vision for your walk with Him.

In what part of your life do you most easily model Jesus? In what part of your life do you struggle modeling Jesus?

_____

_____

_____

Straight from God

Iron sharpens iron, and one man sharpens another. (Proverbs 27:17)

This verse shows God planned for our relationships to refine us. What positive effect has your marriage had on your character? What character weaknesses have been exposed through your marriage?

_____

_____

_____

For Your Marriage (choose one or more)

Share today's Straight from God verse with your spouse. (Call, text, email, discuss.)

Consider the idea your marriage is a long-term work of God. What challenges does this idea present? What benefits does this idea present? (Call, text, email, discuss.)

How would your mate answer these questions? (Ask.)

What are ways in which you and your mate model Jesus? (Share, discuss.)

What are ways in which your mate feels you each model Jesus? (Ask, discuss.)

Ask God to help you recognize and welcome moments that appear to be conflicts but are actually opportunities for refinement, then listen for His response. (Share, discuss.)

NOTES

_____

_____

_____

_____

_____

_____

_____

_____

_____

_____

_____

_____

Week Five, Day Five

A Bottom-Line Litmus Test in Marriage

Over the years, I've discovered many Scriptures that don't directly address marriage in their text, yet absolutely address marriage in their application. James 4:17 is one such Scripture: "So whoever knows the right thing to do and fails to do it, for him it is sin."

I believe this Scripture holds a powerful key for every Christian marriage.

As a believer, I have a scriptural mandate to do the right thing. Period. Always. In every situation. In every relationship. Especially in my marriage—no matter what my spouse does.

Which means I love when I don't feel loved or feel like loving. I give when I don't feel like giving, when I don't think it's really my turn to give, when I feel like all I've done is give and give and give. I encourage, when I desperately need encouragement. I pray for my husband when I'm tired. I listen to him when I'd prefer doing something else.

I believe this Scripture cuts to the heart of my responsibility in marriage. It makes me primarily accountable to God in my marriage, rather than to my mate. It puts my behavior in light of my own relationship with God, rather than the condition of my relationship with my mate.

As God has worked on me, worked in me, broken me, and grown me in Him, I've come to a place where He demands I use this Scripture as a litmus test for my actions in my marriage. I fail, I do, sometimes often in a short period of time.

Still, this verse provides many benefits for me. Considering my actions and motivations in light of this verse helps me clear away the dross in my mind. It helps me quickly get clarity about my behavior. It helps me look past circumstances, petty offenses, and stupid disagreements that used to take up hours of my time and leave my heart, and my husband's, bruised.

James 4:17 helps me focus on what's important, not necessarily what's in my face at that moment.

What about you? If the vagaries of Ephesians 5 and other biblical passages on marriage leave you confused or frustrated, try applying James 4:17 to your marriage. Use it as your bottom line. Your quality control. I promise you'll enjoy the results.

Just for You

Think—reread this week's Scripture passage. Consider the practical good things you do for others every day (doing laundry, cooking meals, mowing the yard, offering a smile or a kiss, feeding and rocking children, taking out the garbage).

How do these good things resemble practical things God does for you?

_____

_____

_____

Thank God—for the simple guideline in James 4:17, that we can keep from sinning by doing the good things we know we should do.

Ask God to bring to mind more good things you can do for your spouse and marriage. What is He saying to you?

_____

_____

_____

Take—strength to do these things from the promise of God's provision.

What do you need from God to do the good things He's asking you to do?

_____

_____

_____

Straight from God

For it is God who works in you, both to will and to work for his good pleasure. (Philippians 2:13)

This verse tells us even the desire to do good comes from God's work in us. If you are weary of doing good things for your mate and marriage, tell God. Write a prayer to Him about your weariness and ask Him for the desire to continue doing His will.

_____

_____

_____

For Your Marriage (choose one or more)

Share today's Straight from God verse with your spouse. (Call, text, email, discuss.)

Thank God for His goodness to you. Share those thoughts with your beloved. (Call, text, email, discuss.)

What good thing has your mate done for you recently? (Share, show gratitude.)

What good thing can you do for your mate today? (Ask.)

Ask God to reveal any roots of weariness in your marriage and listen for His response. (Share, discuss.)

NOTES

_____

_____

_____

_____

_____

_____

_____

_____

_____

_____

_____

_____

_____

_____

_____

_____

_____

_____

Quick Connection for the Weekend

Impact

Which topic from this week affected you the most? Why?

What your marriage vows mean   Why marriage is hard
Men and women aren't opposites   Always doing good
Cultivating kindness and forgiveness

_____

_____

_____

Deeper Connection

What part of Psalm 34 did you find most encouraging?

_____

_____

_____

How can this truth help you grow in God and in your marriage?

_____

_____

_____

What part of Psalm 34 did you find most challenging?

_____

_____

_____

What do you need from God to meet this challenge?

_____

_____

_____

Several verses in Psalm 34 describe being in trouble but finding help and refuge in God. Believers are not exempt from trouble. Sometimes we have trouble from within (battles in ourselves), trouble in our marriage (between husband and wife), and from without (external circumstances beyond our control). What trouble has your attention right now?

_____

_____

_____

Verses 8–14 give instruction for how to stay out of trouble, or at least avoid making more trouble for ourselves. Which of these verses do you find most difficult to obey?

_____

_____

_____

Discuss how following these instructions can help you hide in God and find refuge in Him.

_____

_____

_____

Evidence of God's goodness is all around us. Even amidst trouble, if we are honest and try, we can find something to thank God for. And, often after a trial, when we look back, we see God was at work even during our toughest circumstances. Describe a time you thought God was absent or inattentive, only to later discover all God accomplished through those circumstances.

_____

_____

_____

Carry it Forward

What is one thing you need from your mate to help you meet this week's greatest challenge?

_____

_____

_____

What is one thing you can do for your mate to help him with this week's greatest challenge?

_____

_____

_____

Pray Together:

Heavenly Father, Thank You that your work in us continues through easy times and difficult times. Thank You that even the tension in our marriage reveals our need of You and provokes us to seek You. Help us remember our position and relationship with You first, in conflict and in peace. In Jesus's name. Amen.

OBSTACLES

Scriptures for this Week (Matthew 6:5–15)

[5] *"And when you pray, you must not be like the hypocrites. For they love to stand and pray in the synagogues and at the street corners, that they may be seen by others. Truly, I say to you, they have received their reward.* [6] *But when you pray, go into your room and shut the door and pray to your Father who is in secret. And your Father who sees in secret will reward you.* [7] *"And when you pray, do not heap up empty phrases as the Gentiles do, for they think that they will be heard for their many words.* [8] *Do not be like them, for your Father knows what you need before you ask him.* [9] *Pray then like this: Our Father in heaven, hallowed be your name.* [10] *Your kingdom come, your will be done, on earth as it is in heaven.* [11] *Give us this day our daily bread,* [12] *and forgive us our debts, as we also have forgiven our debtors.* [13] *And lead us not into temptation, but deliver us from evil.* [14] *For if you forgive others their trespasses, your heavenly Father will also forgive you,* [15] *but if you do not forgive others their trespasses, neither will your Father forgive your trespasses."*

Week Six, Day One

Overcoming Weaknesses

As I stated before, (and regularly post my woes about on Facebook) I'm not the greatest cook.

There are like, a half dozen things I'm pretty good at cooking. The rest is hit or miss, and usually involves setting off the smoke alarm, opening windows, and the use of several fans.

No, I'm not kidding.

I just can't get the hang of it! If I never had to cook another meal for the rest of my life, I wouldn't miss it. My idea of heaven includes room service for every meal, delivered in dishes I don't have to wash.

And while I'm daydreaming, I'll add that the streets of gold in my heaven are lined with tables of desserts. Fabulous, decadent, oozing chocolate, caramel, and cherry sauce desserts that—wait for it—I didn't cook. Woo-hoo!

While I've not yet mastered the art of cooking, I have learned a few things about myself and marriage over the past thirty-seven plus years.

One: I'm more carnal than I ever believed.

I'm selfish. It's the bald-faced truth. I want what I want, sometimes before I realize I want it, and I get frustrated when I don't get it. I can get upset about something I don't yet have, and easily project that frustration onto my husband.

Guess how many times I've had to apologize for that.

Two: I can be terribly shortsighted.

When I'm bothered by something, my field of vision shortens and narrows, until I can barely see an inch in front of my nose. I lose all perspective, and often that perspective is re-established only after God thumps me on the head.

Guess how many times I've had to apologize for that.

Three: Loving and giving make me happier than not loving and giving.

I have to fight my inherent selfishness, but when I do successfully set it aside, I'm happier than if I'd scrunched my face and pouted in the corner like a spoiled child.

I've had to learn to be kind. Learn to be loving and giving. Learn to be gracious. The "sweet gene" in me was so wounded during my childhood it needs on-going therapy.

Guess how hard I've had to work to cultivate graciousness.

As I look back over my marriage, I see many times when my weaknesses made a mess. But thank God, every time I try to be a better me, every time I try to change, He's right there as my living example and has everything I need.

What are your weaknesses? What damage have those weaknesses done to your marriage?

What if you spent a month, or a year, working with God to change those habits, so you never again have to clean up the mess you usually make in that area?

I challenge you: Dare to make a list of your weaknesses. Lay them before God. Search Scripture for insight and truth. Work with God to change those habits.

A year from now, you might look in the mirror and see a different you, and an improved marriage. Wouldn't that be cool? Wouldn't that be a miracle of God?

Just for You

Think—reread this week's Scripture passage. Consider the fact your weaknesses aren't a surprise to God.

How can this truth help you receive God's love and forgiveness when you need it?

_____

_____

_____

Thank God—your greatest weaknesses can still be overcome with God's help.

What weakness is God helping you overcome?

_____

_____

_____

Take—strength and direction from God the next time you struggle with a weakness.

What weaknesses are most difficult for you to discuss with God?

_____

_____

_____

Straight from God

But he said to me, "My grace is sufficient for you, for my power is made perfect in weakness." Therefore I will boast all the more gladly of my weaknesses, so that the power of Christ may rest upon me. (2 Corinthians 12:9)

This verse tells us how we are to view our weaknesses. We should see them as areas where God's power can be manifested in and through us. Often when we recognize an area of weakness, our first response might be try to hide it or overcome it in our own strength. What manifestations of God's power would you most like those you know and love to see at work in you?

_____

_____

_____

For Your Marriage (choose one or more)

Share today's Straight from God verse with your mate. (Call, text, email, discuss.)

What weaknesses do you have that negatively affect your marriage? (Share.)

What weaknesses does your mate have that negatively affect your marriage? (Ask.)

What would be evidence of God helping you overcome these weaknesses with His power? (Share, discuss, pray.)

What would your mate see as evidence of God helping them overcome their weaknesses with His power? (Ask, discuss, pray.)

Ask God to teach you how to let His power manifest in your weakness and listen for His response. (Share, discuss.)

NOTES

_____
_____
_____
_____
_____
_____
_____
_____
_____
_____
_____
_____
_____
_____

Week Six, Day Two

The Power of an Apology

I wanted sooooooo badly to be a mother. There was a period of time I chose to help in the church nursery simply to be near infants. There was even a period of time merely looking at a pregnant woman made my eyes fill with tears.

I still remember the moment I carried my first son across the porch and through the back door of our home. I thought *I am totally, completely responsible for this little guy and everything he needs*.

Inside, I freaked out a bit.

Fast forward about four months. My baby had been screaming for five or six hours. I did everything I could think of. I tried putting him in the swing. I tried running the vacuum. I checked his diaper. I gave him his pacifier.

My husband walked with him. Patted him.

I sang to him. Rocked him.

At my wit's end, I finally left him in his crib and sat outside his bedroom door sobbing. And I confess, I had quite the ugly thought toward my child. *You have ruined being a mother for me*. It shames me to admit, but I think I yelled it.

My nerves were frayed and looking forward I saw nothing but sleep deprivation and failure.

My husband walked over. He was probably afraid to, but he knelt beside me. "When was his last bottle?"

I looked at him.

"Did we feed him when we should have?" Stephen asked.

By that time, I'd missed not one, but two feedings.

My poor little boy was beyond hungry, because I'd completely forgotten to feed him.

I think I apologized for hours, while feeding him, of course.

Getting into a mother's mindset didn't come easily for me. I wanted to be a mother. I wanted to be a great mother. But the weight of constantly being conscious of another, the burden of always thinking about what the baby needed, was a difficult adjustment for me.

I never forgot another feeding. That experience taught me exactly how sorry I could be when I'd failed as a parent.

The pain of knowing you missed it and totally screwed up is beyond mortifying. Our kids look at us expecting us to know better. Be better. Do better. When we mess up and know we've hurt our children or our mate, it's a terrible feeling.

Being a perfect parent or spouse isn't what's most important. What's most important is being a repentant and ever-growing parent or spouse.

I've had to apologize to my children and my husband many times over the years. Some of those apologies were tough and gut-wrenching, because I knew I'd made a terrible mistake. I let selfishness take over. Or frustration. Or impatience.

Or I simply didn't make myself remember God had entrusted my children to me to point them to Him. I didn't make myself remember I'd promised before God to love my husband.

Whatever the reason, the apology was only the beginning. My behavior needed to change. Rather than hiding that growth from my husband and family, I now choose to share it with them. When I'm struggling, I tell them. When I need a minute to get myself together, so I don't react and behave badly, I try to take that minute and tell them why I need it.

A real apology is like painkiller and antibiotics to an infected wound. It takes out the sting and helps the wound heal.

Today, do you owe your spouse or children an apology? Do you need to give them the gift of healing for their hearts? The gift of a better relationship with you?

I know it's hard. I know that sometimes looking at our failures makes us want to hide or even puke, and never again look another human being in the face.

I beg you not to hide your failures. Talk to God about your weaknesses, learn from them, and share that with your mate and family. They all have their own weaknesses, too.

One of the greatest gifts we can give others is the method and the motivation to fix their mistakes in their relationships. If we model that in our marriage by apologizing to our beloved when we should, we'll be a living example of repentance and restoration.

Just for You

Think—reread this week's Scripture passage. We all make mistakes, either by accident or with careless intent.

Are you good at admitting your mistakes? Why, or why not?

_____

_____

_____

Thank God—for loving us first despite our sinful nature.

Describe the first time you confessed sin to God and received salvation.

_____

_____

_____

Take—comfort knowing God is quick to forgive when we repent.

Are you quick to forgive when others apologize to you? Why, or why not?

_____

_____

_____

Straight from God

For godly grief produces a repentance that leads to salvation without regret, (2 Corinthians 7:10a)

This verse shows us "godly grief," or conviction, leads us to repentance. God helps us see our need to confess our sin and receive salvation. However, embarrassment can keep us from admitting our sin to God and others. And the enemy likes to use pride to keep us from apologizing when we should. What do you need to confess to God today?

_____

_____

_____

For Your Marriage (choose one or more)

Share today's Straight from God verse with your mate. (Call, text, email, discuss.)

What apology do you need to give your beloved? (Ask.)

What apology do you need from your beloved? (Share.)

Pray as individuals and together asking God's forgiveness. (Share, discuss.)

How can you depend on God's power to forgive each other? (Share, discuss.)

Ask God to help you create a habit of being quick to repent and listen for His response. (Share, discuss.)

NOTES

_____

_____

_____

_____

_____

_____

_____

_____

_____

_____

_____

_____

_____

_____

_____

Why Some Christians Skip Church on Father's Day or Mother's Day

Many don't realize or notice, but Father's Day and Mother's Day can be two of the most painful Sundays for an ever-growing group in our society. Not because of deceased parents, but because of absent or hurtful ones.

For those who were physically or emotionally abandoned by a parent, sitting through a Father's Day or Mother's Day sermon about how terrific parents are can be traumatic or completely impossible. I know one young woman who hasn't attended church on Father's Day for over a decade. She simply can't sit through it despite the fact she's attended the same home church since birth. Her father attended that church, too—until he left her mother.

A scenario like this can be just as uncomfortable and confusing to children: When mom and dad were married to each other, the family sat together in church every Sunday. Now they're divorced, and the child rotates Sundays, or better yet, services. Obviously, on Mother's Day he sits with his mother. And on Father's Day, with his father. The parents believe this keeps continuity for their child. They don't understand they may have just split worship right down the center, making it difficult for their child to ever again view church as neutral or safe territory.

What's worse? You ask. *Our home isn't happy. Wouldn't it be better to divorce than live fighting and mistreating each other in front of our children?*

You're asking the wrong questions. This isn't an either/or situation—stay together miserable or divorce for the sake of your and your children's sanity. That's what the devil wants us all to believe. Scripture allows for divorce in certain cases, but in general, God offers a third and righteous option.

Don't divorce for your sanity. Don't stay married for your children. Instead, fix the marriage. Begin with personal repentance, then proceed with personal sacrifice.

If when you were engaged or early in your marriage someone had asked *Would you die for your spouse?* you probably would have said *yes*, right?

Consider this: Die daily for your mate. Live in constant submission to God and His work in you, letting the fruit of that work spill out to others starting with your mate.

If you have children, don't take them to church, pray over your meals, then live with your spouse as if you don't know God. Rather, love each other. Love, love, love, love, love each other. Let your children see that love, feel that love, its authenticity and its intensity. Show them God's love working through you to mend what's broken, to rebuild what is rubble.

This is true humility before God. Being willing to die daily for my mate and seeking to live like Jesus. Only then will my marriage be the testimony God planned all along.

Just for You

Think—reread this week's Scripture passage. Your children, your family, and your friends are watching your walk with God.

What do you want them to learn about God as they watch your life?

_____

_____

_____

Thank God—for Jesus's example of giving His life for us and submitting His will to the Father.

What resistance do you have to giving your life for your mate, family, or submitting to God's plan for your marriage?

_____

_____

_____

Take—notice of God's example to love the unlovable, give first, give all, and always stay with us.

What circumstances in your marriage cause you to want to leave—physically or emotionally?

_____

_____

_____

Straight from God

"By this all people will know that you are my disciples, if you have love for one another." (John 13:35)

When we're unhappy, unsatisfied, or underappreciated in marriage, loving others can be difficult. During those times, we can easily forget our responsibility as believers. We are to model God's love in our everyday lives, especially in our marriage. When do you find it hardest to show love to your spouse? Why?

_____

_____

_____

For Your Marriage (choose one or more)

Share today's Straight from God verse with your mate. (Call, text, email, discuss.)

Other than Jesus, what is the best human example of love you have seen? (Share.)

Othe than Jesus, what is the best human example of love your spouse has seen? (Ask.)

What can you do during tough times to keep your heart open to your mate? (Share, discuss.)

What can your mate do during tough times to keep their heart open to you? (Share, discuss.)

Ask God to reveal any area you have closed your heart to Him or your mate, then listen for His response. (Share, discuss.)

NOTES

_____
_____
_____
_____
_____
_____
_____
_____
_____
_____
_____
_____
_____

Week Six, Day Four

My Marriage Had Two Broken Legs (Part I)

If you've ever watched a soap opera, a reality show like *The Bachelorette*, or even the old classic *Dallas* (admit it, you've seen at least part of an episode of one of these) you've seen these phenomena in the relationships depicted on screen:

One: habitual negative reactions.

Two: assuming the other person's motives.

Unfortunately, I've seen this behavior in many marriages. And today, I want to focus on habitual negative reactions—something I've been terribly guilty of, especially in the early years of my marriage.

Here's the cold reality. Living reacting negatively will kill a marriage. Did you get that? It will *kill* a marriage.

Always reacting negatively to my husband's behavior is like trying to walk around on two broken legs. It simply won't work, and I'll only add more pain to the pain I already feel.

Here's why: The dynamic creates a hostile environment that breeds animosity and lacks personal accountability. My mate did A, so I will now do B. My mate and I become enemies rather than teammates.

Marriages cannot withstand this habit.

If I do something stupid to offend or hurt my husband, then he does something harmful in return, we simply create a vicious cycle that leads us nowhere. The hurt is compounded, and eventually we're both making excuses for our current behaviors, because neither of us can remember what started the whole mess in the first place.

Sound familiar?

I'm not saying we can't keep our humanity in a godly marriage. I'm not saying our feelings don't matter and our mate is allowed to hurt us in any way, any time they choose. I'm not saying we can't protect ourselves if there's real and true danger. I'm saying that in a godly marriage, you and I don't have permission from God or the right to perpetuate conflict. Living reacting negatively perpetuates conflict.

We're called to be peacemakers. We're called to love each other.

We're called to be a living example of Christ and the Church.

When you find yourself in the position of constantly reacting, ask yourself these questions:

Why do I feel so threatened?

Why did my mate's actions or comments hurt me so badly?

How does this situation make me feel? What does it make me think or believe?

What is the truth God wants me to remember in this moment of conflict?

When conflict comes, viewing our reactions and the roots of those reactions through the truth of God's character and His Word will help diffuse that conflict.

Do you live reacting negatively in your marriage? Have you fallen into habits and cycles that damage your marriage?

I challenge you to address this pattern by discussing it with God, considering the truth of His Word, with the help of the Holy Spirit, and examining the character of Jesus.

Bring Jesus into your next conflict. *Be like* Jesus in your next conflict, and let God grow joy and fulfillment where there has been only pain and destruction.

Just for You

Think—reread this week's Scripture passage. Jesus was never controlled by the actions of others, but He did only what God the Father wanted Him to do.

How much of your time do you spend reacting to circumstances or the actions of others?

_____

_____

_____

Thank God—He does not react to us as we deserve, but rather extends mercy and grace to us.

What negative reaction do you usually have when you're hurt or upset?

_____

_____

_____

Take—directive from Scripture that your marriage is to be a picture of Christ's relationship with the Church.

In what ways do your reactions follow or disobey this directive?

_____

_____

_____

Straight from God

Know this, my beloved brothers: let every person be quick to hear, slow to speak, slow to anger; [20]for the anger of man does not produce the righteousness of God. (James 1:19–20)

This verse is often used with regard to verbal communication, but it can also be applied to what we think, how we process, and how we respond in everyday life. "Quick to hear" means listen first and listen completely. "Slow to speak" means think first and don't rush to judgment. "Slow to anger" means take the time to seek the truth and understand first, without going straight to conflict. Of these three phrases, which behavior comes most easily to you? Which behavior is most difficult for you? Why?

_____

_____

_____

For Your Marriage (choose one or more)

Share today's Straight from God verse with your spouse. (Call, text, email, discuss.)

When has your own negative response caused a problem in your marriage? (Ask/share, discuss.)

When has your mate's negative response caused a problem in your marriage? (Share, discuss.)

How can you help each be "quick to hear, slow to speak, (and) slow to anger," especially when in conflict? (Ask/share, discuss.)

Ask God what hinders you from consistently seeing your mate as a brother or sister in Christ and listen for His response. (Share, discuss.)

NOTES

_____

_____

_____

_____

_____

_____

_____

_____

_____

_____

_____

_____

_____

_____

_____

_____

Week Six, Day Five

My Marriage Had Two Broken Legs (Part 2)

Yesterday I mentioned soap operas, the way they depict relationships, and the danger of habitually reacting negatively to my mate's behavior.

When we consistently choose to react negatively to our mate's behavior, it's like our marriage has two broken legs. We can't go anywhere or do anything without a lot of pain and hassle.

Today we look at another marriage killer that can lock us into a harmful cycle—assuming motives.

Whenever I've flipped channels on the television and landed on a soap opera, I've had to laugh at how many times I've seen this scene:

Main character's relationship is in trouble. Main character stands at a window or stares at a photo of significant other. Main character's thoughts in a voice-over reflect a dissection of significant other's behavior and possible motives.

The speculation that ensues is ridiculous and usually includes a lot of *what ifs?* It includes a lot of analyzing previous conversations for double-meanings, innuendos, loopholes, and deception.

I was several years into my marriage before I realized I often assumed my husband's motives. And, no, I didn't stare out windows or spend long moments gazing at photos.

For me, this knee-jerk reaction happened in a thousandth of a second, every time I felt unloved, unsafe, unimportant, or taken for granted. I mistakenly attributed meaning and motives to my husband's behavior, based on previous experiences during and before my marriage.

Sound familiar?

When was the last time you were hurt by something your mate did, only to later discover that wasn't the intent *at all*?

When was the last time a simple miscommunication took place, and the enemy tried to convince you your marriage was doomed?

When was the last time you took what could have been an inconsequential misunderstanding and blew it up into World War III?

I've done it.

I've done it. Apologized. Felt stupid. And done it again.

This behavior is tough to change for those of us who carried this habit and the hurts that caused it into our marriage. If you learned to blame others, to always be on the defensive, to believe you aren't important, or if you were betrayed, passed over, or rejected—assuming motives might be a reason your marriage seems to be full of conflict.

I challenge you. Ask God to help you see if you have this habit. Ask Him to reveal any damage you've done to your mate and marriage, so He can help you fix it.

Then, spend time and effort with God working on yourself. Figure out why you attribute a particular motivation to one or many of the same actions. Most likely, you'll find a wound or hurt you brought into your marriage.

That's your target. Let God heal it. Ask Him to teach you how to behave differently and watch love grow where there has been conflict.

Just for You

Think—reread this week's Scripture passage. Consider all the habits and traits you brought to your marriage.

Which ones have been beneficial? Which ones have been harmful?

_____

_____

_____

Thank God—He can heal all wounds and hurts from your past.

What habits and traits mentioned above were learned from a painful experience? What habits and traits mentioned above were learned from a pleasant experience?

_____

_____

_____

Take—relief from God that as He reveals harmful habits, His intentions are for your good.

What wounds do you need God to reveal and heal today?

_____

_____

_____

Straight from God

Do not be conformed to this world, but be transformed by the renewal of your mind, (Romans 12:2a)

Every hurt and wound we experienced before marriage, and every bad habit and negative belief we learned affects how we perceive others—especially our mates. This is why Scripture commands us to be transformed by having our minds renewed. We have to let God heal our wounds, change our habits and our beliefs, so we can think clearly. So we can deal with what is true now, rather than projecting what we experienced in the past onto today. What wounds and hurt, habits and beliefs from your past, have caused you to assume motives in your marriage?

_____

_____

_____

For Your Marriage (choose one or more)

Share today's Straight from God verse with your mate. (Call, text, email, discuss.)

What assumptions on your part have caused problems in your marriage? (Ask, share, discuss.)

What assumptions on your mate's part have caused problems in your marriage? (Share, discuss.)

How can you avoid making inaccurate assumptions about each other? (Share, discuss.)

Ask God to reveal incorrect assumptions you have about Him and listen for His response. (Share, discuss.)

NOTES

_____

_____

_____

_____

_____

_____

_____

_____

_____

_____

_____

_____

_____

_____

_____

_____

Quick Connection for the Weekend

Impact

Which topic from this week affected you the most? Why?

Overcoming weaknesses   Two broken legs (part 1): negative reactions
The power of an apology   Two broken legs (part 2): assuming motives
Why some Christians skip church

_____

_____

_____

Deeper Connection

What part of Matthew 6:5–15 do you find most encouraging?

_____

_____

_____

How can this truth help you grow in God and in your marriage?

_____

_____

_____

What part of Matthew 6:5–15 do you find most challenging?

_____

_____

_____

What do you need from God to meet this challenge?

_____

_____

_____

In verse 9, we are told to remember God as our Father and address Him as such. By doing so, we acknowledge His authority over us and our relationship with Him. What benefits do we experience because God is our Father? What responsibilities do we have because God is our Father?

_____

_____

_____

In verse 10, we are told to pray for God's will to be done. Just because my wants, goals, and dreams seem good to me, doesn't mean they're God's will. When have you desired something you thought was good, only to later learn it wasn't good? What did that experience teach you about God and His will?

_____

_____

_____

Verses 11–15 mention the idea of forgiveness five times. Granting forgiveness when others hurt us can be difficult. Yet, God demands that we forgive—we must hand the responsibility of remembering the offense, and of extending judgment and appropriate punishment, to God. Describe a time when forgiving was difficult. Have you been able to forgive? Why, or why not?

_____

_____

_____

Carry it Forward

What is one thing you need from your beloved to help you meet this week's greatest challenge?

_____

_____

_____

What is one thing you can do for your beloved to help them with this week's greatest challenge?

_____

_____

_____

Pray Together:

Heavenly Father, Thank You for teaching us to pray. For reminding us that you have our best interests at heart and that you know our needs even before we ask. Help us find peace and rest in You, even while waiting for You to answer our prayers. In Jesus's name. Amen.

DAILY WISDOM

Scriptures for This Week
(Galatians 5:16–26)

[16] *But I say, walk by the Spirit, and you will not gratify the desires of the flesh.* [17] *For the desires of the flesh are against the Spirit, and the desires of the Spirit are against the flesh, for these are opposed to each other, to keep you from doing the things you want to do.* [18] *But if you are led by the Spirit, you are not under the law.* [19] *Now the works of the flesh are evident: sexual immorality, impurity, sensuality,* [20] *idolatry, sorcery, enmity, strife, jealousy, fits of anger, rivalries, dissensions, divisions,* [21] *envy, drunkenness, orgies, and things like these. I warn you, as I warned you before, that those who do such things will not inherit the kingdom of God.* [22] *But the fruit of the Spirit is love, joy, peace, patience, kindness, goodness, faithfulness,* [23] *gentleness, self-control; against such things there is no law.* [24] *And those who belong to Christ Jesus have crucified the flesh with its passions and desires.* [25] *If we live by the Spirit, let us also keep in step with the Spirit.* [26] *Let us not become conceited, provoking one another, envying one another.*

Three Priceless Gifts That Don't Cost a Penny

Years ago, when our finances were tighter than tight and I couldn't even afford to buy Stephen a card for Valentine's Day, I began discovering three priceless gifts I can give my mate every single day.

First, praying for him. Not flippant, surface, or habitual prayer that simply repeated a list of his wants. And certainly not the list of what I wanted God to change in him.

No, God began teaching me about intercession. About praying for Stephen solely for his benefit. Putting myself in his place with job challenges, decisions to make, spiritual growth, extended family challenges, health challenges. Strength in body and mind, restoration, or joy during a difficult season—you name it. Praying for him with the intention and attention I would use if I were praying for *my* biggest, most critical need.

God directed me to take all I knew about Stephen and pray for him as if I were the only person who ever would, because I had a front row seat to see what he faced every day. I was to pray for my husband as if his spiritual life were threatened because in reality, it is. The enemy wants to spiritually destroy us all.

Intercession might not sound romantic. The truth is I feel closer to Stephen when I intercede for him. And because I'm listening to God about how to best pray for him, sometimes God prompts me to share encouragement, truth, or even a joke with him to brighten his day.

The second priceless gift God told me to give was to tell him what I prayed.

This is so important. Letting our mate know what we pray for them is critical. We can write it, text it, call them—whatever. Either way, this gift is rich with benefits to both the pray-er and the pray-ee.

If communicating about spiritual things is new or uncomfortable, this is the opportunity to strengthen that bond. Every marriage needs that.

Third, God instructed me to share two things with Stephen. What I needed him to pray about for me and my personal dreams.

I was so surprised by which one was most difficult! Sharing my needs was easier than sharing my dreams. My needs made sense and Stephen already knew something about most of them.

Sharing my dreams was a different story. Even though he knew I was pursuing writing and speaking to help marriages—of course he knew—speaking aloud to him the particulars of that dream and calling required honesty, humility, and transparency I found difficult. Yet, these three qualities strengthen every marriage.

When God revealed these three habits to me, I realized He was teaching me how to cultivate spiritual intimacy in my marriage—the most important area of intimacy a couple can have. Unbelievers don't have access to this area, but Hallelujah!!—as believers we do.

When this level is activated and embraced, God can heal, change, energize, repair, restore, and redeem any and every area of our marriage we open to Him.

Activating the spiritual level of intimacy in marriage puts problems in their proper perspective, strengthens current bonds, and establishes new ones.

Spiritual intimacy makes everything else work. And it doesn't cost us a penny.

The price is time and intention, humility and grace. But the return? That's guaranteed and priceless.

Just for You

Think—reread this week's Scripture passage. Remember a time you were compelled to pray for someone else's need.

How did praying for another make you feel about yourself? About the person you prayed for?

_____

_____

_____

Thank God—for giving us the opportunity to communicate with Him through prayer.

What prayers are most difficult for you to pray? Why?

_____

_____

_____

Take—strength from knowing God hears your prayers and cares about you and those you care about.

What need in your life is most pressing right now?

_____

_____

_____

Straight from God

Who is to condemn? Christ Jesus is the one who died—more than that, who was raised—who is at the right hand of God, who indeed is interceding for us. (Romans 8:34)

Jesus, your Lord, your Savior, the One who paid the price for your sin, stands by God the Father and continually prays for you. You are always on His mind. He is aware of your needs, and He is aware when you suffer. What do you need from God to face your most pressing need?

_____

_____

_____

For Your Marriage (choose one or more)

Share today's Straight from God verse with your mate. (Call, text, email, discuss.)

What have you prayed for your beloved today? (Share.)

What would you like your beloved to pray for you today? (Ask.)

What keeps you from being sensitive to each other's needs? (Ask, share, discuss.)

If you don't already have the daily habit of praying for each other, how can you create that habit? (Ask, share, discuss.)

Ask God to teach you real intercession for your mate and listen for His response. (Share, discuss.)

NOTES

_____

_____

_____

_____

_____

_____

_____

_____

_____

_____

_____

_____

_____

_____

Four Negative Responses Your Marriage Can't Afford

While in a grocery store checkout line, I overheard a couple's conversation one lane over.

Husband: (Bagging their groceries.) Why do you always buy this?

Wife: I don't always buy that. (Gestures to the bags.) You never pack them right.

Husband: Well. I won't do it anymore. You can do it your own [expletive] self, next time.

Wife: (No response.)

My heart ached for them. I couldn't help thinking if they speak to each other like that in public when others can clearly hear, what worse, cruel things do they say to each other behind closed doors? Obviously, they'd had this conversation and others like it before.

And as I glanced back at them, I could tell by their expressions that neither would apologize, neither would reach for the other. They both felt their responses were justified based on past experiences, past behaviors, frustration, or hurt.

They were older than me. It's possible they'd been married fifty years or more. But those few short sentences gave tremendous insight into the condition of their relationship. I wished I could go back in time, befriend them early in their marriage, and share with them all God continues to teach me about marriage. I wished I could have given them insight. And encouragement. And warn them of four responses their marriage couldn't afford, so that maybe, just maybe, they could have avoided the path that brought them to this place in their relationship.

True, they might not have listened. I sure hope you do. And I hope you'll share this with everyone you know who's married or ever hopes to be married. I wish someone had told me before I brought these words into my marriage, words that can indicate or create an Intimacy Barrier.

An Intimacy Barrier is any habit, tendency, belief, or thought pattern that inhibits intimacy between me and my mate. In plain speak, it's the stuff that gets in the way of us being close, comfortable companions.

And just like having a fever, or a sore throat, or aches and pains can be signs I'm getting the flu, these four signs indicate disharmony—an Intimacy Barrier—lifting its ugly head in my marriage. These can manifest in spoken or unspoken communication. What I mean is, even if I don't *say* them, if I *think* them, I've probably got a problem.

The four negative responses my marriage can't afford are:

Always.

No.

Never.

And the most dangerous: Silence.

Is there a time and a place for each of these? A time when they're appropriate and positive? Absolutely. But when I use them in a negative way, these responses often indicate I've made a judgment about my mate, and I'm reacting to past behaviors.

I've closed my spirit. I'm allowing no room for my mate to change and grow in a positive way.

I'm depending on the past, rather than the present, to control my future.

Always, *no*, and *never* are bad enough. They cause wounds, and they often manifest wounds. But when the contention between us yields a distance filled with cold silence, we are at even greater risk. A wall has been built. A barrier is in place.

Regarding what subject, in what area of your marriage, do you already have these negative responses lined up and waiting? They're sitting there, in place, because the pattern of dissension has been established. Like a dance you know by heart, a routine you go through without even thinking about it.

Don't let your relationship stay that way. Don't let even one tiny corner of your marriage fester with this love-killing poison.

Rewrite your love story now by throwing out negative responses, so something as simple as a trip to the grocery store isn't a date with disaster.

Just for You

Think—reread this week's Scripture passage. Remember a time you were blamed for something you didn't do.

How did that make you feel? How did that affect your relationship with your accuser?

_____

_____

_____

Thank God—Jesus took the blame for your sin so you could receive forgiveness.

What sins do you find most difficult to forgive in others? In yourself?

_____

_____

_____

Take—assurance that you have been reconciled with God through Christ's sacrifice.

How does this knowledge affect your behavior, prayer life, and worship?

_____

_____

_____

Straight from God

Put on then, as God's chosen ones, holy and beloved, compassionate hearts, kindness, humility, meekness, and patience, [13] bearing with one another and, if one has a complaint against another, forgiving each other; as the Lord has forgiven you, so you also must forgive. (Colossians 3:12–13)

When barriers arise between a husband and wife, there is always pain. Sometimes that pain comes because we've been wronged. Sometimes that pain comes because we did wrong. Usually, the pain comes from both directions—my sin and my husband's sin combine to create an awful mess. Healing never comes until both of us apologize and forgive, but one of us has to begin the process. What obstacles do you face when apologizing? What obstacles do you face when offering forgiveness?

For Your Marriage (choose one or more)

Share today's Straight from God verse with your beloved. (Call, text, email, discuss.)

What is hardest for you—asking for forgiveness or offering it? Why? (Share.)

What is hardest for your beloved—asking for forgiveness or offering it? Why? (Ask.)

What help do each of you need from God to overcome these obstacles? (Share, ask, discuss.)

Ask God to show you how to grow compassion, kindness, meekness, humility, and patience, then listen for His response. (Share, discuss.)

NOTES

_____

_____

_____

_____

_____

_____

_____

_____

_____

_____

_____

_____

_____

_____

_____

Week Seven, Day Three

Avoid a Common Communication Problem—If Necessary, Consult a Dictionary

I once had a conversation with the father of a teenage girl. She'd used part of her savings (with her father's permission) to buy her new boyfriend a Christmas present. The problem was, in the father's opinion she'd deliberately disobeyed him by spending too much money on the gift. He was furious with her.

On the other hand, the young girl was devastated. Not only because her father was upset with her, but because she thought she'd shown maturity in her gift choice. She'd chosen a gold chain, rather than a video game or a goofy T-shirt. The disagreement escalated to the daughter wanting to leave home. She felt she could never please her father. After a few minutes talking with him, I understood what had happened.

The father: I told her to be reasonable. The gift she bought cost too much money, which makes it inappropriate.

Me: Did you tell her how much she could spend?

The father: No. She should have … known.

Me: So, she made a mistake, in your opinion a bad decision, but she wasn't deliberately disobedient, was she?

His expression told me he realized what he'd done and how the miscommunication had happened. He wasn't specific when giving his permission, so the teenager had bought what was reasonable and appropriate *to her*.

Different words mean different things to different people, even husbands and wives.

Many of us remember President Bill Clinton's famous line while being questioned about his relationship with Monica Lewinsky "… it depends upon what the meaning of the words *is* is." I'm probably not the only person who wondered what Hilary's definition of *is* is.

Anyway … A misunderstanding can be defined as "We *missed* an *understanding*."

A communication glitch can happen between me and my husband over a word as simple as *soon*—as in how quickly a task should be done. Or the idea of *a little*—as in how much should be spent on an item. Or even *want*—as in something that might be fun to have, versus what we really need.

We have experienced serious misunderstandings, sometimes marriage-threatening misunderstandings over a word or phrase. Not because one of us is being petty, but because we didn't make sure we each meant the same thing when using a particular word or phrase.

When differing definitions cause communication problems in marriage, ending the dissension can be difficult. Yet, if I pay attention and am aware of the patterns, I can limit or eliminate fruitless conflict.

What are the tricky words, phrases, or concepts in your marriage? Make clarifying those ideas a priority, so a potential conflict can be avoided. Don't let a simple word or phrase damage your marriage.

If necessary, consult a dictionary. Just be certain you both have the same version!

Just for You

Think—reread this week's Scripture passage. Consider the conflicts between you and others throughout your life.

How many came from simple misunderstandings?

_____

_____

_____

Thank God—He knows your heart and your intentions.

What feelings or needs are hardest for you to express to God? Why?

_____

_____

_____

Take—comfort knowing God is always at work for your good.

What feelings or needs are easiest for you to express to God? Why?

_____

_____

_____

Straight from God

If one gives an answer before he hears, it is his folly and shame. (Proverbs 18:13)

When we're in the midst of a misunderstanding, it's easy to want to restate our case, try to persuade the other person to our perspective, and stop listening. This verse clearly tells us the danger of not listening before we speak. Asking for clarification and listening to the answer can be time consuming but is usually fruitful, even if we have to ask more than once. What subject is most difficult for you and your mate to discuss? Why?

_____

_____

_____

For Your Marriage (choose one or more)

Share today's Straight from God verse with your beloved. (Call, text, email, discuss.)

What conversations do you try to avoid in your marriage? Why? (Share.)

What conversations does your beloved try to avoid in your marriage? Why? (Ask.)

What negative and positive history do you have with confrontation? (Share, discuss.)

What negative and positive history does your spouse have with confrontation? (Ask, discuss.)

Ask God to help you create a unified strategy for handling confrontation and listen for His response. (Share, discuss.)

NOTES

_____

_____

_____

_____

_____

_____

_____

_____

_____

_____

_____

_____

_____

Are You Looking for Advice in the Wrong Place?

Remember the scene from the film *Indiana Jones: Raiders of the Lost Ark* where Jones and Sallah realize the Nazi's staff headpiece had markings only on one side? Which meant their staff was the wrong height? Which meant they were digging in the wrong place?

The Nazis had taken over an area of the desert. They had men and machines working every day to locate The Well of the Souls, which was thought to contain the Ark of the Covenant. They were desperate. They were intentional. They had money to invest in the project and worked tirelessly toward their goal.

Still, their efforts were in vain. Because their staff was the wrong height, when sunlight shone through their staff to a location on a map of the city, the highlighted location was incorrect. They were digging in the wrong place because their information came from an incorrect source.

The place to start when beginning, building, or reconstructing a marriage is God and His Word.

Your parents may have the best marriage you've ever seen. You can ask for their input and benefit from their encouragement. But copying them in everything isn't healthy. Your parents aren't you and your mate. They don't have the same background, problems, personalities, or callings.

To build a healthy marriage, we must start and end with God.

Yes, we can benefit from questioning others, listening, and observing. I hope you learn from this devotional and all the stories I share here.

But in your home, where it's just you and your beloved, you two have to find the techniques and habits that work for you, as God leads, directs, and empowers.

If you have trouble expressing your feelings, that's probably exactly what God wants to teach you. If you have trouble being quiet and listening, that's probably exactly what you need to do. If you tend to place blame, you'll need to learn to extend grace and be merciful. If you tend to live as a martyr, you might need to learn to receive more or deal with your pride.

I admit, I came to marriage with all of these challenges in some form. God convicts and confronts me about them in direct correlation to my relationship with Him and His work in me at the time. My walk with God isn't the same as yours or even the same as my husband's. We each walk a unique path.

That's why we have to be careful about copying specific techniques we learn from others. What might work in another marriage won't take into account my heart or motives. It won't account for my mate's needs, history, strengths, weaknesses, or spiritual and personal growth. Copying others is like sawing off the tree limb we're sitting on. Yes, the saw will do the job, but because of where we are in relation to the saw and the limb, we can be badly hurt.

You and your mate are to learn about each other and learn to love each other as God wants you to love. This process is specific to you as the Holy Spirit leads. Just as the individual journeys you and your mate walk with God are unique, your marriage is, too.

Do you look to others for ideas too often?

Do you justify your own poor decisions based on the actions or advice of others?

Have you simply not put in the effort to think with God and learn from God?

As with your relationship with God, the condition of your portion of your marriage depends on you and only you. This truth holds both a responsibility and a gift. If we righteously handle our responsibility, we can enjoy the gift.

Just for You

Think—reread this week's Scripture passages. Think about the fact your decisions affect every area of your relationship with God and your mate.

What area of your relationship with God would you like strengthen? Why?

_____

_____

_____

Thank God—that as He works in you, He is also working in your marriage.

What area of your marriage would you like to be stronger? Why?

_____

_____

_____

Take—strength from your relationship with God and His Spirit at work in you.

What godly traits is God building in you now? How can those traits strengthen your marriage?

_____

_____

_____

Straight from God

Two are better than one, because they have a good reward for their toil. ¹⁰ For if they fall, one will lift up his fellow. But woe to him who is alone when he falls and has not another to lift him up! ¹¹ Again, if two lie together, they keep warm, but how can one keep warm alone? ¹² And though a man might prevail against one who is alone, two will withstand him—a threefold cord is not quickly broken. (Ecclesiastes 4:9–12)

This passage shows us "two are better than one" and lists several benefits of having a partner: Greater return for work. Help when we fall. Warmth—both physically and emotionally. Even stronger is the couple who so entwines their lives and marriage with God—"a threefold cord is not quickly broken." In what areas have you successfully entwined God in your marriage?

_____

_____

_____

For Your Marriage (choose one or more)

Share today's Straight from God verse with your spouse. (Call, text, email, discuss.)

In what area have you seen spiritual growth in your spouse? How has that affected your marriage? (Share.)

In what area has your mate seen spiritual growth in you? How has that affected your marriage? (Ask.)

In what areas do you each need to increase your dependence on and connection with God? (Share, ask, discuss, pray.)

Ask God to help you reach for Him and your mate in areas of your life and marriage you are alone, then listen for His response. (Share, discuss.)

NOTES

_____

_____

_____

_____

_____

_____

_____

_____

_____

_____

_____

_____

_____

_____

Week Seven, Day Five

How Can I Stay in Love?

The following conversation took place at one of my bridal showers.

My aunt: Shellie, you look so happy.

Me: I am happy. I can't wait to be married. We really love each other.

My aunt: Just wait a few years.

Wow, right? As I considered her marriage—the way she treated her husband and the way he treated her—I couldn't help wondering if the chicken or the egg had come first. Did they treat each other poorly because they'd fallen out of love, or had they fallen out of love because they treated each other poorly?

Since my own parents' marriage had ended in divorce, I was already prone to worrying about falling out of love with my soon-to-be husband. I wanted to know *how* to stay in love. How to always *want* to be near my mate. How to *care* about him. How to care if I suddenly seemed to *stop* caring.

Falling in love is easy. Staying in love takes intent, effort, and choice.

When I first started studying and learning about God's plan for marriage, the passage in Ephesians 5 became my cornerstone. It's my starting place for all I've learned about marriage. A thriving, healthy marriage depends on me learning about God's character, how He loves, how to be loved by Him, and how to cultivate my relationship with Him, then duplicating those habits in my marriage.

Think about how you feel spiritually when you forget God. When you're not intentional about paying attention to your relationship. When you make no effort to grow. When every choice you make takes you further away from God.

You feel distance. You feel alone and uncared for. You might feel forgotten. Because you didn't invest.

Yes, in our spiritual lives, some investments give an instant return while others take years or decades. Sometimes we wait for a while before we see fruit for our efforts.

But if I let myself forget my husband …

If I put no energy into my marriage …

If I don't choose him over all others …

… my marriage will not thrive, regardless of what he invests in our relationship.

God invested all when He sent Jesus to die for our sins, yet many receive no benefit from that sacrifice because *they* won't invest in a relationship with Him.

Is there an area of your marriage you've left forgotten and untended? Are you sharing a home, children, and a mortgage, but your marriage is a barren wasteland? Have you become indifferent to your mate?

I challenge you: Begin to invest in your marriage as never before. Take what you've learned from your relationship with God and apply it to how you grow your marriage.

Just as it's possible to stay in love with Jesus, it's possible to stay in love with your mate. Let God be your marriage coach, your example, and your source. The time spent with Him will spill over to your marriage in every best way.

Just for You

Think—reread this week's Scripture passage. A relationship with God is available to everyone.

When did you first become aware of your need for God and His forgiveness?

_____
_____
_____

Thank God—for the love that provoked Him to send Jesus to die for your sins.

Describe your salvation experience.

_____
_____
_____

Take—relief for your heart (your sin is gone), your mind (you can learn to think like Christ), and your emotions (God can heal every wound), from Christ's complete work on the Cross.

What manifestation of God's love and character means the most to you today?

_____
_____
_____

Straight from God

"For God so loved the world, that he gave his only Son, that whoever believes in him should not perish but have eternal life. [17] For God did not send his Son into the world to condemn the world, but in order that the world might be saved through him." (John 3:16–17)

God's love is a force unlike any other. It reaches us despite our sin. When we really see God's love, we recognize our tremendous need. When have you seen God's love change a life? How has God's love changed your life?

_____

_____

_____

For Your Marriage (choose one or more)

Share today's Straight from God verse with your mate. (Call, text, email, discuss.)

What would you like God's love to change in your marriage? (Share.)

What would your mate like God's love to change in your marriage? (Ask.)

What struggle in your marriage is most perplexing to you? (Share.)

What struggle in your marriage is most perplexing to your mate? (Ask.)

Pray as individuals and together asking God to help you recognize, understand, and extend God's love to each other. (Share, ask, discuss, pray.)

Ask God to reveal any area where you have chosen to feel condemned rather than loved by His offer of salvation and listen for His response. (Share, discuss.)

NOTES

_____

_____

_____

_____

_____

_____

_____

_____

_____

_____

_____

Quick Connection for the Weekend

Impact

Which topic from this week affected you the most? Why?

Three priceless gifts   Looking for advice in the wrong place
Four negative responses   How can I stay in love
Avoid common communication problems

_____

_____

_____

Deeper Connection

What part of Galatians 5:16–26 do you find most encouraging?

_____

_____

_____

How can this truth help you grow in God and in your marriage?

_____

_____

_____

What part of Galatians 5:16–26 do you find most challenging?

_____

_____

_____

What do you need from God to meet this challenge?

_____

_____

_____

In verse 16, Paul encourages us to "walk by the Spirit." Some translations say "walk in the Spirit." What do you think it means to walk by or in the Spirit? Name someone whom you believe exemplifies this verse. In what ways do they exemplify it?

_____

_____

When God's Spirit lives in us, our lives will change. Over time, our lives will show the fruits listed in verses twenty-two and twenty-three: "love, joy, peace, patience, kindness, goodness, faithfulness, gentleness, self-control." Why do you think "love" is listed first? Which of these are more difficult for you to manifest? Which are easier for you to manifest? Why?

_____

_____

When our carnal flesh wars with the Spirit's work in us, we cannot be passive. We have to choose who will be our master—our flesh, or the Spirit. Paul uses the word "crucified" to describe the definitive choice we make when we choose to follow the Spirit. What difficult choices have you made to follow the Spirit rather than your flesh? What impact did those choices have on your relationship with God? On your marriage?

_____

_____

Carry it Forward

What is one thing you need from your mate to help you meet this week's greatest challenge?

_____

_____

_____

What is one thing you can do for your mate to help them with this week's greatest challenge?

_____

_____

_____

Pray Together:

Heavenly Father, Thank You that your Spirit is always at work in us. Thank You that the fruit of that work helps our marriage. Help us yield to the Spirit in all things. In Jesus's name. Amen.

ABOUT THE AUTHOR

Shellie Arnold is an author, speaker, and Biblical Marriage Strategist. She truly believes any marriage can thrive if both husband and wife will listen to God. *Joined by God* is her first seven-week devotional for couples. *Love and Loving*, her second seven-week devotional, will be released in early 2025.

Shellie's novels depict the perfect storms in marriage—what happens when a husband's and wife's weaknesses hit head-on and they're both left wondering if anything can be salvaged. Her first three novels follow three marriages within the same church. They are:

The Spindle Chair
Sticks and Stones
Abide with Me

Find Shellie and her soon-to-be-released podcast *Christian Marriage Uncensored* at www.shelliearnold.com.